Founded in 1964 by John W...
Voices: Journal of the Ameri...

Editor:
Kristin Staroba, MSW | *kristin.staroba@gmail.com*
1201 Connecticut Ave., NW, Ste. 710
Washington DC 20036

Graphic Designer:
Mary de Wit

Business Manager:
Lisa Kays
1800 R Street NW #C-8
Washington, DC 20009

International Consultant:
Jacob Megdell, PhD, Canada

Emeriti:
Penelope L. Norton, PhD, *Immediate Past Editor*
Doris Jackson, PhD, *Editor Emerita*
Tom Burns, PhD, *Editor Emeritus*
Jon Farber, PhD, *Editor Emeritus*
Monique Savlin, PhD, *Editor Emerita*
Edward Tick, PhD, *Editor Emeritus*
E. Mark Stern, PhD, *Editor Emeritus*
Vin Rosenthal, PhD, *Editor Emeritus*

Associates:
Hallie S. Lovett, PhD, *Contributing Editor*
Bob Rosenblatt, PhD, *Intervision Editor*
Barry Wepman, PhD, *Poetry Editor*
Ruth Wittersgreen, PhD, *Poetry Editor*

Editorial Review Board:
Carla Bauer, LCSW
Lee Blackwell, PhD
Brooke Bralove, LCSW-C
Peggy Brooks, PhD
Grover Criswell, MDiv
Susan Diamond, MSW
Molly Donovan, PhD
Nicholas Emmanuel, LPC
Rhona Engels, ACSW
Stephanie Ezust, PhD
Pamela Finnerty, PhD
Natan Harpaz, PhD
Stephen Howard, MD
Susan Jacobson, MMH
Nicholas Kirsch, PhD
Judy Lazarus, MSW
Matthew Leary, PhD
Kay Loveland, PhD
Laurie Michaels, PhD
Don Murphy, PhD
Giuliana Reed, MSW
Ann Reifman, PhD
John Rhead, PhD
Murray Scher, PhD
Avrum Weiss, PhD
Sharilyn Wiskup, LPC

VOICES: THE ART AND SCIENCE OF PSYCHOTHERAPY (ISSN 0042-8272) is published by the American Academy of Psychotherapists, 230 Washington Ave Ext, Suite 101 / Albany, NY 12203.

Subscription prices for one year (three issues): $65 for individuals PDF only; $85 for individuals PDF & print copy; $249 for institutions. Orders by mail payable by check: 230 Washington Ave Ext, Suite 101 / Albany, NY 12203. Orders by MasterCard or Visa: call (518) 240-1178 or fax (518) 463-8656. Payments must be made in U.S. dollars through a U.S. bank made payable to *AAP Voices*. Some back volumes may be available from the *Voices* Business Office.

Change of Address: Please inform publisher as soon as a change to your email address is made. Send change of email address to aap@caphill.com.▼

Journal of the American Academy of Psychotherapists

VOICES

THE ART AND SCIENCE OF PSYCHOTHERAPY

Every orgasm makes a contribution to world peace.
—Donald Lathrop

Journal of the American Academy of Psychotherapists

VOICES
THE ART AND SCIENCE OF PSYCHOTHERAPY

Silence   Summer 2018: Volume 54, Number 2

Voices: Journal of the American Academy of Psychotherapists		i
Table of Contents		v

Editorials

Silence, Sexuality and Spirituality in Psychotherapy	Elizabeth Field	1
Voices of Silence	Kristin Staroba	2

Articles: Spirituality and Sexuality

The Sexually Unspeakables:		
A Conversation Between Two Sex Therapists	Steve K.D.Eichel & Anni Tuikka	4
The Intersection of Sexuality and Religion:		
Changing the Conversation	Kate Ott	15
A Preacher's Legacy	Raymond J. Ball	20
I'm OK If We're OK:		
Men's Fears of Women in Intimate Relationships	Avrum G. Weiss	24
Interview with Ellen Fox	Elizabeth Field	34
Sexuality and Spirituality: One Man's Journey	John Rhead	41
Befriending Silence in Therapy	Bruce Knight	44

Articles: Silence

Gina's Wisdom	Steven Abell	55
Silence: Healing the Hidden Darkness in Psychotherapy	Omar "Nick" Bustos	61
Ambushed	William Boylin	74
Introduction of Dana Jack	Penelope Norton	76
Silence Sounds	Dana Jack	78
How I Speak	Noah Meyers	85
The Road Goes Ever On and On	Kristin Staroba	88
I Got It	Catherine B. Clemmer	92
Unspeakable	Scott Baum	96
The Business of Silence: Communication Without Words	Kristie Nies & Mike Geringer	100
Closings: Part 2	Ellen Weber Libby	107

From the Archives

Hearing the Melody: The Silence of Psychotherapy	Kenneth Wapnick	68

Silence

Poetry

Longing To Be Read	Ray Ball	**23**
Untitled	Mitchell Foy	**33**
My Patients Think I'm Crazy	Maury Joseph	**106**

Calls for Papers

Memory, Meaning & Story	Deadline January 15, 2019	**113**
The Ghost in You	Deadline April 15, 2019	**114**
The Geometry of Place, The Tangled Roots of Home	Deadline August 15, 2019	**115**

Voices

Subscribe to Voices	**116**
Guidelines for Contributors	**117**
The American Academy of Psychotherapists	**118**

On the Cover:
Darwin's Secret
2016, Sean Williams
Editorial Photography Within: Mary de Wit

©2018 by the American Academy of Psychotherapists, Inc.
Published three times per year.
Cover Design: Mary de Wit
Design and Production by
Mary de Wit | in2Wit®, llc
AAP Web Site:
www.aapweb.com

Editorials

Silence, Sexuality and Spirituality in Psychotherapy

Elizabeth Field

ELIZABETH E. FIELD, MA, LMFT, LCAS, earned her undergraduate degree in psychology, minoring in philosophy and religion, from ASU in 1996. She obtained her graduate education at ASU in marriage and family therapy in 1999. Since her graduating year she has attended AAP as her primary continuing education training. She has practiced psychotherapy since 1998. Currently she has a full-time private practice in Charlotte, North Carolina. Her most recent interests are sex therapy and couple's therapy. For her, these areas are an opportunity to bridge her previous work in addiction and trauma with the art of healing by creating healthy relationships. She is married and has two sons (12 and 4 years old) and a yellow lab-mix dog who inspire her daily.
clt.therapy.elizabethfield@gmail.com

I found a silver bowl engraved with my parents' wedding date when I was 13 years old. An extraordinary find, on one level, given the hostility my mother always held for my father. Extraordinary on another level, in that the date was barely 6 months before my birth. Of course, I had to ask my mom all about it! And a dialogue began, around the truth of my origin story. Discovering that silver bowl (not kept for sentimental reasons) revealed the truth about my inception and the reason for my parents' marriage.

Statistically, I should not have been conceived. My mother had an IUD inserted to avoid this inconvenience, after the birth of her second son in 1968. "I was born with a double uterus," I recall my mother offering my 13-year-old self, by way of explanation. I prefer my aunt's version: "Your mother's uterus is in the shape of a heart." It was this unusual shape which gave me the safety I needed to start my life. The OBGYN assured my mother she would abort naturally when they retrieved the IUD. The doctor was wrong. My parents were left to deal with the life they had created in their momentary bliss with each other. I think of myself as a "love child." I believe I am a miracle. Aren't we all miracles?

We all begin in the darkness and silence of our mother's womb. At conception, we all contain the ingredients necessary to become the people we are ultimately meant to be. Yet, the womb is a hostile environment, so not all these early lives become people. The fact is, many do not, and many things can happen along the way to interfere in one's development. Though the story of my conception could be a crude one, as I was neither planned nor wanted, I was indeed created out of my parents' mutual, though short-lived, desire for each other. My mother was a newly divorced mom of two young boys. My father was a Cuban immigrant who had served in the U.S. military and graduated from the local university and was beginning his career in law enforcement. My parents were just people, neighbors, who were meeting their sexual needs.

This is where spirituality or faith stories become particularly relevant in my origin story. My father was raised in a strict Catholic home and my mother in a strict Baptist home. Their faith-based home lives led them to believe they had no choice but to keep me and additionally to enter a marriage with each other. So, is it any wonder that I became a marriage and family therapist? I have been bringing people together from the moment my life began. This is what bubbles up for me when I ponder silence in psychotherapy. It is not just the secrets we carry, but the beginning of life's desire to be, to become, to develop into who we are, starting with very tiny essences of life, in the dark, in silence, where there are no words, only movement, joining and separating. It is for me a fight, and a right, to live despite the odds or what authority states.

So, for this issue of *Voices*, I looked for authors to write on the themes of sexuality, spirituality and psychotherapy, and found some journeyers who were willing to go there with me.

Kristin Staroba

KRISTIN STAROBA, MSW, has a private practice in downtown Washington, DC, seeing adults in individual, couples, and group psychotherapy. She has presented numerous times at AAP meetings and salons and is the incoming president-elect of the Academy. She is currently the editor of this journal, and steps down from that post in 2019.
kristin.staroba@gmail.com

Voices of Silence

Not long ago, a client taught me a lesson about keeping quiet. Usually engaging, insightful, gregarious, this young woman came in to her early-morning appointment, grabbed the throw I keep folded nearby, plunked down on my sofa, and declared, "I'm going to take a nap, ok?" After a moment, I said, "Sure." She laid down, settling, and closed her eyes. She peeked at me briefly once or twice and then seemed truly to fall asleep. Bemused, I wondered whether to quietly work on something else, or even to let myself nod off. After a few minutes sitting still, though, I felt electrically alert. Realizing that the session was taking place regardless of her sleeping or waking, I felt calm and attentive. I was able to stay present, simply taking her in, noticing my breath and hers. The hour passed quickly, and she woke up a few minutes before it was to end. We smiled. She got up, gathered her things and bid me good-bye until the following week.

Months later, we were talking more about our relationship as she prepared to end our work and move across the country for a job. The nap came up as an example of trust. It had been a rare moment for me of being invited to silently keep vigil over her vulnerability. My acceptance let her stay undefended. It was a sweet exchange. I'm not sure of all of the nap's meaning or significance, but our silence held the relationship in a way talking could not.

This issue of *Voices* explores two different aspects of silence. In the first half, guest editor Elizabeth Field brings writers from multiple backgrounds to consider how psychotherapy relates to spirituality and sexuality. This is a rich inquiry into both. I thank her for her diligent and creative efforts to present a true smorgasbord of perspectives.

Anni Tuikka and Steve Eichel carry on a conversation about what is "unspeakable" in their practices as sex therapists. Sexuality educator Kate Ott brings an irreverent perspective to teaching in a religious context. Ray Ball recounts his own painfully intense struggle with a preacher father.

Avrum Weiss borrows from his online column to consider how men are afraid of women. Guest editor Elizabeth Field interviews Ellen Fox, a sex therapist whose office is inside a church. With a hat tipped to his mother for starting him off in the right direction, John Rhead explores how each of his parents influenced his experience of sexuality and spirituality. Bruce Knight applies his own experience of problematic sexual behavior to treatment that is spiritually based.

The second half of this issue tackles the theme of the 2018 AAP Institute & Conference, "Sounds of Silence: Working the Edges of the Unspoken." First, Steven Abell offers the case of "Gina," a girl who teaches him that healing is sometimes a silent engagement. In a philosophical vein, Nick Bustos draws on Paul Wapnick's use of *A Course in Miracles* to explore how silence is the medium of client-therapist connection; we reprise a Wapnick article from the archives as well. William Boylin offers a vignette of an encounter he and his brother had with Carl Whitaker that broke their silence.

Drawing straight from the I&C, we present here in written form a panel introduced by former *Voices* editor Penelope Norton and led by plenary speaker Dana Jack, who created the Silencing the Self Scale. Three of four scheduled panelists—Noah Meyers, Kristin Staroba, and Catherine Clemmer—write about their experiences of being silenced.

Two other I&C presenters look deeply into their personal stories of silence. Scott Baum shares thoughts about patients organized as borderline or schizophrenic. Kristie Nies and her partner Mike Geringer tackle positive and negative uses of silence by couples.

Finally, Ellen Weber Libby concludes her examination of retirement begun in the Winter 2017 issue.

As always, poetry and images light our way through the issue. ▼

Steve K. D. Eichel

STEVE K. D. EICHEL, PHD, ABPP, CST, holds degrees and board-certification in counseling psychology and is certified in forensic counseling, clinical hypnosis and EMDR in addition to being an AASECT-certified sex therapist. He presents or co-presents workshops on sexuality, sexual trauma and sex offending at AAP and other national professional meetings, and privately. In his forensic work, he is often called upon to perform risk evaluations of individuals charged with sex offenses.
steve@dreichel.com

The Sexually Unspeakables:
A Conversation Between Two Sex Therapists

When Anni Tuikka and I were invited to write an article for the "Silence" issue of *Voices*, we felt both honored and intimidated. Sex therapists hear so many secrets and other "unspokens"; it would be difficult to know how and where to start and when and where to end. So many unspoken stories! As we discussed the possible ways of handling our assignment, it was Anni who suddenly realized that rather than converse about our writing, perhaps we should write about our conversing. The result is this edited transcript of two lengthy conversations we had about what does and does not get spoken when dealing with sexuality.

Tuikka: Steve, what would you say are the most common "sexually unspeakable" topics for patients—or you—that you have encountered in your work as a sex therapist?

Eichel: From the male point of view, I'd say performance issues, erectile dysfunction, and delayed ejaculation are the most common things that men have difficulty talking about. Also, desire discrepancy between partners. Various versions of non-monogamy, including affairs, also bring into daylight deep struggles with secrecy and angst. Another huge unspeakable topic is incest, whether parent-child or between siblings or other close relatives.

What about you? What do you run into?

Tuikka: From my perspective, probably the low-desire and no-desire issue is the most common and difficult to discuss and navigate in relationships. Another one I run into frequently with women is physical discomfort or pain during sex. It's less about secrecy than simply about people not knowing how to talk about these kinds of negative sexual things. I think what makes it difficult to talk about is that the individual feels like there's something wrong with them and that it's shameful. And I'm sure we've both run into sexual trauma like rape, harassment, and bullying that takes a strong therapeutic alliance and sensitivity to address. Then there's BDSM (bondage and discipline, dominance and submission, sadism and masochism), in other words, any kind of non-vanilla sexual activity.

Eichel: Most uncommon sexual interests—paraphilias—are definitely on the list of "unspeakables." And let's not forget trans and other gender issues.

Tuikka: Fortunately, our society, and really the whole world, is at a point of radical change regarding genders other than male–female.

Eichel: So, let's get into it...

Low Desire

Eichel: What were you saying about the men and women with low or no desire that you've seen?

Tuikka: It may come up in a phone call when I ask what prompted them to call. The person who has the lower desire often has a very difficult time bringing it up. If it's a male, there's a lot of hemming and hawing before they get to it. I would say in men's cases, it's about their sense of masculinity, not feeling that they are man enough if they don't want sex as much as their partner. If this is in a heterosexual couple, the man may perceive that the woman doesn't respect him as a man. And often he is unfortu-

Anni Tuikka

ANNI TUIKKA, LPC, is a psychotherapist, certified sex therapist, and certified supervisor of sex therapists and counselors. She is in private practice in Atlanta and works primarily with individuals and couples seeking to enhance their sexual fulfillment. She frequently utilizes trauma treatment modalities (EMDR, Brainspotting). She holds master's degrees in psychology from Georgia School of Professional Psychology and in education from the University of Tampere, Finland. She presents on sexuality topics at AAP and elsewhere.
atuikka@sent.com

nately correct. If it's the female who has lower libido, it's also about feeling inadequate or, "I'm not enough." Or the woman may be frustrated that the man pesters her and can't seem to be able to just stop being so sexual.

Eichel: Right.

Tuikka: So that's why it stays silent until the other partner or I ask a question that breaks the dam. It often takes a long time to work the low-desire partner to a point where the shame allows them to mention it, not to mention figuring out what it's about, the roots, and how to start changing it. Obviously, as sex therapists we help them change what they want to change, but it's not that simple. Giving various gradual exercises, such as sensate focus, doesn't help if we don't know the roots and the family and cultural background.

Eichel: It's interesting that the men I have worked with who complain about low desire have generally been younger men, so that's different than what most people would expect. I see a fair number of college students, and I've heard these complaints from men in their mid-30s. They are usually very hesitant to admit it—especially with their partner present. It eventually comes out in a later couples session or in individual sessions. Sometimes they're more willing to admit that they have low desire in general, rather than a lack of desire for their partner, which may be an even bigger secret.

Tuikka: Let's go back to a married couple with low or no desire... A lot of our work is in defining it, in figuring out what they really want sexually, or what they don't want. What is it that doesn't work in the relationship? We have to move away from finding fault, from the view that somebody's doing something wrong, from seeing that they are inadequate. That view doesn't help the patient. I often hear the question, "What am I doing wrong?" The no- or low-desire partner feels in their being that they are not doing anything wrong, yet sex doesn't work. Of course, people often learn, especially from porn, that you just look at the other person and smile, and then you start taking clothes off and everything works just fine. In real life, that's not how it works much of the time, especially in long-term relationships. I'm not saying that it never works that way; it certainly can work at times, but less and less often the longer the partners are together.

Fantasies

Eichel: You know that I am not anti-pornography, but I am puzzled and curious... Young men today are using pornography very, very differently than my generation did. We didn't have access the way young people have it now.

Tuikka: Not 24/7.

Eichel: Yeah, 24/7 and anywhere they may be.

Tuikka: Yes, novelty wearing off is certainly one thing, so they go for more and for broader variety. But I agree with you about the changing role of pornography. I'm not even saying that porn in itself is bad for these young people, but they are too often using it in an unhealthy way. Younger men in their early 20s to early 30s—the generation for whom video pornography has been available 24/7 ever since they were 12—are in the process of building their arousal template, in other words, what they need in order to be turned on sexually. When teenagers use constant novelty in video porn as their primary way of getting aroused, and in their first times masturbating, they don't know that it's not sustainable on a continuous basis if they want to be sexual with a real-life person. They don't know that it's not helpful to seek more intensity and more novelty every time.

Eichel: That's right.

Tuikka: These young men haven't really learned anything about relating to partners from porn videos. Nothing about emotions, connection, touch, eye contact, etc. On the videos, it's just fucking, and that doesn't work with live partners, so there's often confusion that negatively impacts desire. The man can be confused because his penis doesn't work as well with live women as it does when masturbating with videos.

Eichel: What in your experience are people keeping secret as far as their fantasies go? I mean fantasies that, if they were expressed, might actually be useful.

Tuikka: Well, one thing that is very difficult to talk about—I usually intentionally "stumble" on it—is including a third person or even more in their fantasies. Patients immediately look at their partner with thoughts like, "Oh my God, now he/she is thinking that I want to sleep around and that I'm having an affair and that I'm no longer attracted to my partner." That's definitely one difficult fantasy that would be helpful to talk about. Another thing is that a partner whose sexual behavior preference has been normative and "vanilla" typically has a hard time hearing something that is less vanilla from their partner. Again, that immediately goes into, "You mean sex with me is not enough, it's not exciting enough?"

Eichel: Right.

Tuikka: So they don't want to bring it up. It takes quite a while. I have worked out a way to include fantasies in my couple work. Patients create their fantasies at home, first just short snippets, say a scene and a location, then gradually incorporate more elaborate sexual elements. Over time, they do get more relaxed when they see that their partner is actually turned on. Or they get interested in learning what turns themselves on in fantasies.

Fantasies are so wonderfully simple in a way, because you can skip a lot. You don't have to try to figure things out in fantasies: such as how you got there, how much it costs, and who takes care of the kids. You can skip all that. Just snap your fingers and it happens: You can be in the Blue Lagoon somewhere.

Eichel: Yes, one of the big things I run into—although it's rare because I don't think most people are willing to admit it, even to a therapist—is what folks in the sex addiction field call a "euphoric recall." Now the sex addiction folks use this term very negatively, whereas I think at times it can be extremely positive.

The Sexually Unspeakables

Tuikka: Could you explain that?

Eichel: That's when you're with your current partner, but you're fantasizing about a prior sexual experience, usually with a different person. You're recalling a past sexual experience, and it's causing a kind of sexual euphoria.

Tuikka: Experience that is triggered by the current relationship or current situation, or just in general?

Eichel: Just in general. It can be really upsetting when that kind of fantasy comes out, and therefore I can understand why it almost never does. One of the biggest secrets not talked about is when, let's say, Jim is having sex with Jane, but he's remembering having sex with Sarah, a previous lover.

Tuikka: And also, something that is secret in fantasies that is harder to get to, is wanting something sexual that the partner doesn't want, or that the couple hasn't tried. For instance, fantasizing about a BDSM scene when all the couple has ever tried is vanilla sex.

Eichel: Yes.

Tuikka: When it comes up, the vanilla partner often asks the person who is fantasizing, "Is this normal?" Also, with BDSM or threesomes or group sex, acts that are not unusual at all in fantasies, it's hard to talk about them in relationships.

Eichel: Yes, absolutely. You're familiar with Barry McCarthy's (2015) term, *bridge to orgasm*, right?

Tuikka: Very familiar.

Eichel: So of course that's something else that's usually very secret, that people don't want to talk about. And they don't necessarily have to talk about it. I think it depends more on one's judgments and attitudes than anything else. I don't know that there's ever been any research on this, but the reality is that for many long-term couples, in order to cross that finish line that separates intense arousal from orgasm, they have to fantasize.

Tuikka: Fantasize about a particular person or sensation to get from the arousal plateau to the Big O.

Eichel: Right. And then, making matters even more complicated, with some of my patients, is the shame and guilt they feel. This winds up being more often with women than with men: the shame and guilt that they feel when the fantasy involves something that is socially unacceptable, like coercion, or incest, or having sex with somebody who would be completely frowned upon by your family or your peers, such as interracial or same-gender sex.

Tuikka: Or being raped.

Eichel: Yes, absolutely. Not only is that not talked about among couples, but I think it's rarely talked about in therapy unless you have a very unusual—and I would say gifted—sex-positive therapist.

Tuikka: Sexual fantasies are hard to work on because they are so private; it takes time to get them out. When the patient brings them up, it's not a simple matter of normalizing and processing it, because it has so much internally-constructed, secretly-built, socially-hushed material around it. The whole scaffolding around the secret is internal, so to work on it in a relational way is hard.

Orgasm

Eichel: Yet another big secret is faking orgasm. Of course, most people are familiar with the idea of women faking orgasm, but there are men who fake orgasm as well.

Tuikka: Yes, it has come up. It's harder for men, especially if they normally ejaculate when they orgasm, which isn't always the case. When they don't orgasm, the women are internalizing it, interpreting it the same way many men do, as "I'm not enough for you," or "You're not into me."

Eichel: Absolutely. And the men interpret it in the same manner, which I think is very problematic. I'm not surprising you here, but certainly as men get older, it becomes far more common to have intercourse for 15 or 20 minutes, but if they haven't had an orgasm, sometimes the sensitivity of the penis decreases. After a while they just figure, "I'm not going to have an orgasm," and a lot of men see that very negatively. They think there's something wrong with them because they're not cumming in the traditional sense, and/or there's something wrong with their partner because she or he isn't making them cum.

Tuikka: Yes. It becomes, "You are responsible for my sexual functioning and my sexual pleasure." That's also where anxiety comes in, specifically for men. They worry about getting and/or maintaining their erection, or whether or not they are going to ejaculate, and at what point. I have been told by male patients that they pray, "Please don't let me lose my erection." I totally understand that it's hard to discuss, especially in the initial conversation, but at the end they say something like, "My goodness, I have never mentioned this to a woman, and I don't know you, and it's hard to talk about." Of course I try to help them hear that they are not alone and that I have heard it a hundred times. And usually that part of the anxiety is alleviated once we get going.

They're less worried about orgasm, although they talk about it as if it were one thing, orgasm and ejaculation, but...

Eichel: There's a fair amount of discussion about the range of orgasmic experience that women have, but I see very little or no discussion about the range of orgasms that men can have. I know some people call it a pseudo-orgasm, or a quasi-orgasm, but they experience a kind of climax without ejaculation.

In my experience, almost no males are aware of that. When they experience it, they interpret it negatively. A lot of men—this is true for young men certainly, but it becomes

The Sexually Unspeakables   **9**

more and more true as men get older—have more difficulty getting and maintaining erections. That, along with possible difficulty achieving orgasm, can cause so much shame and embarrassment that often men will claim that they don't want sex, but what they're really doing is avoiding an experience that they predict is going to be negative.

Tuikka: Thinking of my patients, they might have less of a problem with delayed orgasm, but then of course if their partner is frustrated or sore or something like that, then it becomes a problem, and then it becomes shameful. It isn't necessarily so initially, but when it's associated with negative reinforcement, frustration, disapproval, or "there's something wrong with you" from their partner, then it can turn into shame.

Eichel: I think one of the themes is the idea of engagement: of having your imagination, body, and emotions engaged. I'm not sure how much of that can happen in the current hook-up culture.

What other secrets, or what other silences don't we talk about?

Asexuality

Eichel: There's an area that I think is extremely rare but worth mentioning, and that is asexuality.

Tuikka: Yes. I definitely want to talk about that. People often take it to mean that if somebody doesn't want to have intercourse or doesn't fantasize, they are asexual. That's not necessarily so. They may not know that there can be an erotic element in how they touch, in how they connect. Or how they think about their pet or their goat can be erotic or sexual.

Eichel: You're right.

Tuikka: Even with inanimate objects, there can be erotic and sexual elements, and so when somebody isn't comfortable saying they are in love with their car, they may say that they love their car, but that's different. They may, in this society at this time, say that they are asexual instead, because they do not include *people* in their sexual fantasies and are not looking for that.

Eichel: I hadn't thought of that.

Tuikka: Asexuality is a complicated thing. I'm very careful agreeing when somebody says they must be asexual, because it has such deep, long-term ramifications. They can even program themselves out of having erotic feelings if they hear from the therapist, "Yes, you must be asexual."

When I talk with a patient, without agreeing that a person is or isn't asexual, I ask what makes them say that. After they have described that they don't fantasize, they don't feel like they want to have sex, we then talk about what their experiences with sex have been like, what they have seen, what they have learned, how they view it in movies for instance, and do they like kissing. If they like kissing, that can be erotic or just a social expression of affection.

There's a book called *The Invisible Orientation* by Julie Decker (2015) that describes asexuality. I don't think she is a therapist. She obviously feels strongly about asexuality; she identifies as such. I'm not sure I agree with her very broad definition. It is so hard to define it, and that makes it difficult for me to wrap my head around it. Yet people who wonder if they are asexual are putting a big societal label on themselves. That label can include a lot of confusion and shame. But maybe the label is also necessary for them to get a handle on their sexuality. However, I have noticed that the label often comes from just not wanting to have sex with their current partner or in a particular way the partner wants. In my mind that's not asexuality.

Eichel: That of course would be present in somebody who's asexual, but that's not the one and only criteria. If someone doesn't want to have sex with a partner, but is masturbating, then that's not asexuality.

Tuikka: If somebody has had great sexual experiences in the past and is fantasizing about sex, but they don't want to have sex with their partner, and are not aroused in any way and don't even think about it, it's still hard for me to see that as asexuality. Also, the modern lifestyle, the busy-ness and not making time for relationships... Just this Friday, my patient was explaining that they don't have time for sex. They are focused on their careers, and they don't have children. He's wondering if she's asexual because she doesn't want to have sex. There's no space in their life for sex! That's not asexuality. That's something else.

You know, my hunch is that asexuality is something we will hear people claim more and more. It feels like a trend. Or maybe the zeitgeist is such that it's easier to claim it.

Eichel: That's a good point.

One of the secrets that I run into is using some other explanation to cover up a secret. In other words, you admit one secret in order to cover up secrets that you consider to be even more shameful.

Tuikka: Can you come up with an example?

Eichel: I'm thinking of your example, the person who says that they're asexual and that's why they're not having sex with their partner: "It's not because of anything with you. It's because I'm asexual. I just don't have any sex drive." But really what's going on is that I'm having fantasies about BDSM, for example, and I can't admit that.

Tuikka: That makes me think of another patient. The woman is more or less in love, lusting after and desiring another man, and can't or won't tell her husband. She is the personification of the difficulty we as therapists have to wrestle with: When her husband asked, "Is there somebody else?" she got angry and started backing off. She started saying, "Well, if that's where your mind goes, then let's not talk about it." She got angry exactly because of her secret.

Eichel: And he guessed it.

The Sexually Unspeakables   **11**

Tuikka: Yes.

Eichel: And of course, that only expands the depth of the secret. Then she's got to come up with other secrets to explain the first secret.

Incest

Tuikka: I had a case where I struggled with incest as a secret. I did get some consultation that was helpful. My patient was a woman who, some months into therapy, disclosed that as a child and teenager, she had been having intercourse with her brother, also a minor. It was very hard for her to talk about. Of course, I immediately went to look at the relevant state laws to figure out what I needed to do. I was pretty new as a therapist and felt very uncertain in this kind of situation. I didn't report it because, first of all, it took place a couple of decades earlier, so it was done with. It wasn't ongoing. Also, it was two underage kids. They were both teenagers when it ended. I don't remember who was older and by how much.

Eichel: Were they still sexually involved when you saw her?

Tuikka: No.

Eichel: So this is not a reportable offense in my opinion.

Tuikka: No. It wasn't. But it was one of those unspeakable things. It's not like I had a clear picture from school or from my past experience doing therapy of how to approach this. Incest is very high on the unspeakables list, even putting the legal aspect aside. There is an evolutionary urge to avoid it, but there are circumstances and disorders and all kinds of things that make people still do it.

Eichel: Absolutely.

Tuikka: Have you had incest cases?

Eichel: Yes, I have. As you were talking about that case, I was remembering one that lasted only one session, because, to be candid, I was incompetent. This was a young woman who was in her third year of a clinical psychology program.

In the first session she disclosed having and continuing to have sex with her brother. What was interesting was she said it matter-of-factly, even though she told me she'd never told anyone else about this. Clearly, my reaction was off-putting. I know that she read my face. She pretty much walked out of the session early, and not surprisingly, I never heard from her again. For all I know—and this is one of the things I feel so guilty and awful about—her encounter with me may have ruined her for therapy forever.

Tuikka: How would you deal with that now?

Eichel: I think I would deal with it very differently. I think I would maintain the stance of "less judgment, more curiosity" that I have learned in AAP. I've really taken that to heart in a big way. I think I would handle that case neutrally now, and I would probably say something along the lines of, "I'm wondering, since you told me you've never told anyone else, how you're feeling about the fact that you told me? Did you anticipate any kind of reaction from me?"

When the Therapist Holds the Client's Secret

Tuikka: I have another case that is not a legal issue, but it is an ethical one. I knew that my patient was involved in a relationship outside the marriage, and she was hiding it from the husband. She did talk about it with me alone. I usually meet separately with both partners at least once. In this case it had been more than once; they were trying to figure out whether to stay together or not. That I knew that she was having an affair also became my secret.

Over the years I have come to take the stance that—and I explain it very clearly in the beginning of couple therapy—I don't mind holding secrets when we are working on them and looking for some kind of solution. It doesn't make me unable to work in a balanced way. At least that's how I feel. I also tell both partners in the beginning that if one of them discloses something that in my clinical opinion needs to be discussed, I will ask that person to bring it up in the joint session. I'll be happy to work with that person until they are ready to bring it up. I won't just blurt it out. That's what I told this woman, too. She stated very clearly to me that she did not want her husband to know she was in an affair. We talked about it, and she agreed to put the affair on hold until she knew what she wanted to do with the marriage. I didn't ask her to end the relationship completely, but I did ask her to communicate clearly that it was on hold.

It's such a tightrope. There is no perfect way to deal with this. At least I haven't found it.

I always feel the question inside: "Should she disclose?" Then I look at my own anxieties: "Can I hold onto my anxiety and not push it onto her?" That's where I am with them now.

Eichel: That's an area that I really think is important, and of course it's something that most therapists are going to encounter: In the course of marriage or family therapy, to what degree do you hold someone else's secret?

Tuikka: Like when patients say they fake orgasms? Males and females do that, and it's another secret that they are really ashamed of. Do I disclose that? Why would I do that? What good would that accomplish? We can work on the sexual relationship, on what doesn't work well, without them or me saying that they fake orgasms.

Afterword

Eichel: There is so much to talk about! We could fill the whole *Voices* issue with sexually unspeakable topics and how we face them as sex therapists.

Tuikka: We barely got started with the topics we mentioned in the beginning.

The Sexually Unspeakables

Talking about these things makes me realize how truly sad—and sometimes frustrating—it is that it's so hard to talk about sex in general. I think a lot of these unspeakables could become totally speakable if sex in general were not such a taboo. Can you imagine this society, if talking about sex was as easy as, say, teaching manners to kids? A normal thing.

Eichel: It is hard to imagine. In that kind of society people wouldn't have to lie to their partners about how many sex partners they have had before! You know, men tend to give their partner a lower number than what's true. And there are situations where both sexes give a higher number in order not to sound totally inexperienced.

Tuikka: It blows my mind that in sex, inexperience and ignorance can sometimes be raised into ideals.

Then again, I'm thrilled that I do what I do and get to see every day progress towards more openness and "speakability" regarding sexuality. It makes my day when, every now and then, I get to have wonderful conversations with parents about how to raise their kids in a healthy, sex-positive way, regardless of how the parent was raised. ▼

References

Decker, J. S. (2015). *The invisible orientation: An introduction to asexuality.* New York: Skyhorse Publishing.

McCarthy, B. W. (2015). Bridges to sexual desire. *Journal of Sex Education and Therapy, 21,* 132-141.

The lack of self-awareness in our culture is such that when most people masturbate, they're having sex with a stranger.

—Eddie Reece

Kate Ott

The Intersection of Sexuality and Religion:
Changing the Conversation

DR. KATE OTT is author of *Sex + Faith: Talking with Your Child from Birth to Adolescence* and the forthcoming *Christian Ethics for a Digital Society*. She leads workshops across the country on sexuality and technology issues related to children, teens, young adults, and parents. She is associate professor of Christian social ethics at Drew Theological School and lecturer in practical theology at Yale Divinity School. To find out more about her work visit www.kateott.org. kott@drew.edu

A LACK OF QUALITY, HOLISTIC SEXUALITY EDUCATION IN THE UNITED STATES leaves many of us to seek our own answers and deal with a variety of sexuality-related issues on our own from a young age. In addition, religious teachings have contributed to silence and shame associated with sexuality. In counseling settings, clients might hesitantly raise sexuality issues. However, it is not only clients, but practitioners too, who need to explore their attitudes, values, and histories related to sexuality. Over the past 15 years, I have sought to change the educational approach for seminary students related to sexuality and religion from one focused solely on prevention of sexual abuse and harassment (which is extremely important) to holistic sexuality education. I also educate parents on how to address issues of sexuality, values, culture, and religion in direct, healthy, and holistic ways throughout a child's development. Together, these approaches help us to move beyond silence and shame to sexual health and healing.

I have an unlikely career—being a sexuality educator and Christian seminary professor. It has been a surprising, joyful, and circuitous route. I come to the intersection of sexuality and religion from a Christian perspective and desire to help others work toward healthy, holistic, and justice-based relationships with others and themselves. Participation in religious communities has been an ever-present and influential aspect of my life, even when I have had to make the decision to leave a particular religious community. My faith is the primary foundation for my commitment to social justice and provides the values I try to live out in my relationships. For me, that means faith has a central role in how I understand sexuality and sexual relationships. While this is not true for everyone, religion, Christianity in particular in the US, affects the cultural conversation about sexuality for everyone.

I grew up in a Midwestern Roman Catholic community where we rarely talked about sexuality, and if we did it was usually to reinforce negative comments made about sexual orientation or behaviors. I never considered that sexuality included aspects like sensuality or intimacy because the focus of the sex education class we received only covered the biology of sexual and reproductive health. However, in my church I saw lots of relationships and family structures. There was an implicit message about marriage, family, and commitment. Even though the topic of sexuality was not often explicitly discussed, I was still learning about religious beliefs and actions related to sexuality. Unfortunately, the lack of explicit teaching left me to fill in the gaps.

It was not until I took a few women's and gender studies courses in college that I realized sexuality was part of many aspects of life and deeply influenced by relationships with ourselves and others as well as with social structures. I had the privilege of taking a women's health course that focused on the history of women and gender bias in healthcare and medicine. We used *Our Bodies, Ourselves* (Boston Women's Health Book Collective, 1992) as a core text. During that course, I learned a great deal about my own body, but also about sexuality more generally. Yet, in that context, there was still a disconnect between sexuality and religion as most of my professors blamed religious teachings for the harm many women faced in sexual relationships (and they were partially correct).

I was experiencing an ever-widening divide between two areas of life that seemed to have significant overlap. Something inside me knew the overlap was not solely negative. After college, I attended seminary to do a master's degree. At the time, I thought I would work as a faith-based nonprofit provider related to some sort of community service. It was in seminary that I found many feminist theologians and ethicists who wrote about sexuality in ways that would have surprised my secular undergraduate professors and my religion teachers. Yet, I still wondered why such writings and teachings were not more widely known. Where were all these healthy, positive teachings about sexuality and Christian theology when I was a youth and could have used some guidance?

During this time, I began working as a youth counselor both in a United Methodist church and for a secular nonprofit that dealt with children and youth who were abused and neglected or in the juvenile justice system. I was also starting my own family. The experiences of working with children in so many diverse circumstances raised many questions for me related to sexual abuse and harassment prevention (and healing in the case of some child survivors), healthy family relationships, sexual objectification, and gender bias. I began looking for resources that connected sexuality education and progressive Christian faith-based information. At the time, there was a very strong abstinence-only-until-marriage educational movement in conservative and evangelical church contexts. That type of curriculum has been found to be ineffective (Ott, 2011). Not to mention that it did not fit my context for two very distinct reasons. In youth ministry, I was serving a progressive Christian church that did not share the theological viewpoint of this curriculum. In my social service job, many kids had already been harmed by adult sexual abuse or begun engaging in sexual behaviors themselves. A message of abstinence was not helpful.

I began searching for better resources and started a doctoral program in Christian ethics so that I could research and write about adolescent sexual ethics from that same feminist, healthy, sex-positive perspective I had learned in seminary. I found that in the 1980s, a variety of Protestant and Unitarian Universalist denominations published sexuality education curricula that reflected some of this theological perspective, but these resources were not widely used and many were out-of-date (Haffner & Ott, 2011). Most churches were in a panic to pull together sexual abuse and prevention plans given the media coverage of the sexual abuse scandal in the Roman Catholic Church, as well as a variety of incidents in Protestant churches. Sexual abuse prevention being the overwhelming focus, these plans rarely included sexuality education for the children and youth. The exception to this was *Our Whole Lives* (www.uua.org/re/owl), a lifespan sexuality education curriculum developed by the Unitarian Universalist Association and United Church of Christ. Interestingly, this was also the only curriculum that required teachers to receive training before teaching the curriculum.

I learned quickly that working with youth and families on issues of sexuality meant I needed to do my own work related to my sexual attitudes, values, and history. This was a fairly common training practice for secular sexuality education trainers (Ott, 2013). That is to say, knowledge is necessary to be a sexuality educator, but it is equally important to have a sense of how one's own experiences affect reactions to students, congregants or clients. Given that sexuality can be a very socially charged subject, many individuals experience shame associated with their sexual identity, behaviors, or relationships. The taboo nature of sexuality requires those teaching or counseling on sexuality issues be well-prepared to listen to any subject that might be raised. The youth with whom I worked were very perceptive about which adults they could talk to about sexuality issues and which they would avoid. Those they avoided already had a message prepared and rarely listened to the current struggles or issues from the teen's point of view.

Such an open approach might make perfect sense in a counseling setting. However, in a faith-based setting, leaders and educators often believe it is their role to impart a specific doctrine or rule about sexual behaviors and relationships. For youth, this means they might get very specific instruction, like staying abstinent until marriage, but all their questions about how their bodies change, what to do in current relationships, or what behaviors are okay at different stages of a relationship never get addressed. It also tends to keep the focus of sexuality education only on teens when all ages in congregations need sexuality-related education. Similar to secular comprehensive sexuality education, holistic sexuality education in a faith-based context requires that teachers address their own values, attitudes, and history so they can be more effective, welcoming, and grounded in their role. I am grateful that I was able to work at the Religious Institute (www.religiousinstitute.org). There I received sexuality education training and was able to bring a variety of sexuality issues together with faith-based approaches.

I am no longer a youth minister, but I do spend many weekends at churches across the United States offering workshops on sexuality education and ethics. I am regularly reminded of the discomfort that comes with talking about sexuality, both for parents and youth. Much of the time I spend with parents is twofold. First, I help them clarify the values that are most important to them related to sexuality and relationships: respect, mutuality, kindness, equality, and so on. In a faith-based context we share lots of rules, but rarely talk about our values, which should be the foundation to how we form relationships. Second, I help parents practice answering sexuality-related questions and finding teachable moments so discussions about sexuality are ongoing, rather than one single talk that most kids forget. This means they have to gain comfort putting their values together with sexuality topics (Ott, 2011).

For example, let's say a youth asks, "When is it okay to kiss someone?" It is impossible to list all the scenarios when this might be acceptable, but if we start with values, we can give more guidance. For example, "We kiss people all the time, including friends and family, to show we care about them. That kind of kissing is different than kissing someone we like in a more intimate way. Kissing in a romantic relationship is about care, but it also has to be mutual and consensual, meaning both people want to kiss and both people like the kissing. Kissing is also a way to get closer to someone; you share your physical body in a different way, which means both people have to have respect for each other's body." In a Christian context, I might also add that mutuality, consent, and respect require that we honor the image of God in the other person, so you wouldn't kiss multiple people (cheating) or talk about the kiss with lots of other people (gossiping). That would be disrespectful and you would be dishonoring God in that person.

As for the discomfort that youth experience, imagine having to talk with a complete stranger (me) about sexuality for two or three hours at church. I recently walked into a youth group where three young teenage boys were recounting how their parents forced them to come and how painful this was going to be. After about 30 minutes these three boys were so engaged and talkative, I had to keep asking them to wait until I heard from others. I attribute their shift in comfort level not to "me" but to my training in being open, inviting, and direct in how I address sexuality. Also, when youth realize that I am not going to get flustered, that I take sexuality seriously but also can laugh, and that I care about what kind of relationships they will have now and in the future, they warm up pretty quickly. My approach is to help them clarify their faith values and how those values connect to their sexuality and relationships. If they can do this, they are more likely to make sexual decisions based on their values.

Many adults and youth bring sexuality-related issues to counselors, but they also bring these issues to religious professionals. Sometimes people have been harmed by religious teachings or religious leaders and thus dealing with religion and sexuality is part of healing. Individuals who are struggling with sexuality issues and relate some of the struggle to religious teachings need spaces that will help them work through religious issues toward sexual health and healing. Simply letting congregants know that one is open to discussing sexuality issues can be a major relief to those who are confused or have suffered due to silence and negative teachings. Religious leaders can also partner to address faith-based issues with secular practitioners who can address more clinical issues, as many clergy do not have professional counseling training. My professional sexual ethics courses at Drew Theological School and Yale Divinity School equip students to better address sexuality related issues and make them aware that denominationally required sexual abuse prevention policies have to be accompanied by training of leaders and education for children and youth.

Seminary students, parents, and various practitioners need more than one class or one workshop to adequately address sexuality-related issues. However, one class or workshop often spurs folks to seek out more resources and, at the very least, helps them to be a more welcoming and receptive presence to those who need and want to discuss sexuality-related issues.

References

Boston Women's Health Collective. (1992). *Our bodies, ourselves.* New York: Simon & Schuster. Series, see https://www.ourbodiesourselves.org/

Haffner, D. and Ott, K. (2011). *A time to speak: faith communities and sexuality education*, 3rd ed. Westport, CT: Religious Institute.

Ott, K. (2011). *Sex + faith: talking to your child from birth to adolescence.* Louisville, KY: Westminster John Knox Press.

Ott, K. (2013). Sexuality, health, and integrity. In P. Jung and D. Stephens, *Professional sexual ethics: a holistic ministry approach.* Pp 11-22. Minneapolis, MN: Fortress Press.

Our whole lives. Lifespan sexuality education curriculum series, see https://www.uua.org/re/owl

Raymond J. Ball

RAYMOND J. BALL, BSc, MA, is an Australian refugee in private practice in Charlotte, North Carolina. He offers groups, couples and individual counseling to clients affected by sexual, spiritual, and emotional abuse. He is profane, profligate and occasionally profound. His teenage children remind him regularly he's kinder to total strangers than he is to them. His wife promises "Here Lies Potential" for his headstone. His family of origin only recently realized he no longer lives in Australia.
rayball@ppc1767.org

A Preacher's Legacy

I WAS 14 WHEN I ASKED MY PRESBYTERIAN PREACHER FATHER IF HE THOUGHT (MY) MASTURBATING THREE TIMES A DAY WAS A LITTLE EXCESSIVE. He responded by opening his Bible (New International Version) to Psalm 24 and reading from verse 3:
Who may approach the hill of the Lord?
Who may stand in the place of the Holy?
He who has clean hands and a pure heart!

I was speechless! My father may have read further, spoken more; I don't recall. I have a vague sense of stumbling backwards, struck by the brilliance (or dastardliness) of being rebuked on both the physical and spiritual levels. Not only were my hands not clean but my heart was dark too. This is far worse than I thought!

As I wrestle with my grievance with the church, it has something of this theme to it—an abandoning and shaming quality where its practitioners position themselves in a subtly superior position, and the mood is one of condemnation. A strange place really for a people who are called to "weep with those who weep and rejoice with those who rejoice."

I feel that abandoning element of my father's strategy to this day. He didn't enter into the problem I was seeking to make sense of. I was on my own to figure it out. Far worse though, was the shaming. Did he really believe that making me aware I was unclean and subsequently unable to even approach God, would motivate me to stop? I had experienced this from him before.

I recall waking up six or seven times before the age of 10 completely terrified of "being lost for all eternity!" There was an untethered, lost-in-space, never-ending feel to it. "The door will be SHUT!" he'd thunder as he slapped his hands together in the pulpit, "and you'll be lost for allllll eternity!" It has to be done in a broad Northern Irish accent for its full effect. (My older brother, delightfully adept at the use of humor to deflect the terror about such things, would go further in the imitation: "There will be weeping and wailing and gnashing of teeth, and for those who don't have teeth, TEETH WILL BE PROVIDED!)

I didn't find it funny. I was terrified.

The abused child cannot comprehend the adult as deficient and internalizes the breach in relationship as *their* deficiency. This gives the child something to work on in the near term: if they can just stop doing X, or become very good at Y, maybe the abuse will stop. When does one develop the capacity to discern an incompetent doctor, a corrupt policeman, a lazy teacher, or a harsh and rigid preacher? I was well into my 30s before I ever achieved any emancipation from this framework.

Upon my return to Australia from the US in January of 1995, I wrote my father a single-spaced, 12-page, letter. I was fresh from my graduate degree in counseling and less than a year married to my American bride, who had courageously followed me to the opposite side of the world. I had done my work. I wasn't mad at my father anymore. I was hoping for a more adult relationship. There were some questions I hoped we could engage: "Why did we really leave Northern Ireland and emigrate to Australia? Why did we leave the oldest two kids in the UK?" There was some of my heartache I wanted him to be aware of: "Do you know you broke my heart when you didn't let me travel with our state cricket team to the national tournament, in Adelaide?" And, "Was that decision based on some of the games being played on a Sunday?"

An outpouring of longing: Will you meet me, know me, wrestle with me, Dad? I read and reread it, edited and reworked it for weeks, sanding off every sharp edge. Eventually, I snuck in "under the cover of darkness" and laid it on the desk in his study. This was, after all, where he retreated from us to read his walls of books and write his sermons. I had entered the inner sanctum and laid my offering on the altar. It was full of my longing for more from my father, but equally as much full of longing *for* and *with* him. I hoped he would acknowledge his receipt of it, possibly note the weight and pithiness of the subjects broached and ask for time to consider his response. Mmmm?

The next morning, he walked towards me at the breakfast table, left arm fully extended, holding only the very corner of my letter by thumb and forefinger. He had the look of someone bringing you the dead rat *your* cat left on *their* doorstep! "This is really dark," he said, wafting the pages at me, "I need you to take it back!" Wait! What?

I had that same stumbling-back feeling even though I was sitting down. He laid my offering—my longing for more, my repentance, my offer of forgiveness and hope for restoration—on the table beside me. Frame after frame of snapshot moments between us, opened up all the way back to my question about masturbation. For years I thought *I* was the problem: My hands not clean enough, my motives (heart) not pure enough for you to engage *me*. The narrative I told myself had kept me from facing this reality. Your deficiency! Your inability! Your refusal!

Look at you—wafting the pages of my sacred offering back at me! And calling it "dark" to boot.

It remains an emancipating moment. I was never able to be around my father again without that punched-in-the-stomach, aching, awareness of wanting so much more from him and his refusal to go there with me. For a long time, I thought wanting more and accepting not getting it was what it meant to be a grown-up. I also had to wrestle with my observation that, the more profligate of a prodigal son I became, the more sympathy people had for the preacher! The losses are permanent. The vacuum left is real. And the struggle not to say the deficiency is mine continues.

Dementia swamped all opportunity in the ensuing eight years. I was privileged to be his legal power of attorney, helping facilitate his move to a retirement home and the sale of his estate. It remains one of the favorite seasons of my life—getting to be a grown-up who cared for his father. He came to our house every Tuesday night for dinner and just hung out with us on the weekends. Through the birth of four children in three pregnancies, in five years, we were grateful for the extra pair of hands. I flew home to Perth, Australia, to be present with him at his death in 2007. In what felt like a real gift from him *and* the Father, after four days of his being in a coma, I thought to pray with him, and he died. A Presbyterian minister to the very end, we joke, he was just waiting for someone to close in prayer.

Longing To Be Read

Ray Ball

"Oh! I'm an open book" you said,
"You can ask me anything!"
My:
"What color is your underwear?"
was supposed to give you pause.
But you checked, right there at the table.
Apologizing for having to.

I recall the metaphor,
Watching you bounce out onto
your four-posted stage.
Falling open to familiar passages.

I dive into the narrative,
demanding, tension, drama, intrigue.

And climax.

You hold me there, all legs and arms and fingernails.
Seeming to savor the fleeting and dreading the turning away.

The second time
I check my image in your bureau mirror, you ask:
"Would you like a cup of coffee before you go?"

I leave, wondering,
Who might be up to celebrate my embellishments.
While you? You are somewhere else.
Still longing to be read.

I'm OK If We're OK:
Men's Fears of Women in Intimate Relationships

Editor's note: Part of this content was originally published on the Good Men Project and is republished here with permission from the author.

*Men are afraid that women will laugh at them.
Women are afraid that men will kill them.*
—Margaret Atwood

Avrum G. Weiss

Avrum G. Weiss, PhD, is a psychotherapist and author in Atlanta. The author of two books, Avrum writes a weekly column for www.goodmenproject.com, a website read by more than 3 million people worldwide a month. You can read Avrum's past columns at https://goodmenproject.com/author/agweiss or email him to subscribe to the weekly column.
agweiss@comcast.net

MEN AFRAID OF WOMEN? The idea is so counterintuitive that using "men" and "afraid of women" in the same sentence seems like an oxymoron. It's pretty clear that women are afraid of men, and with good reason. Men hold positions of privilege and power in most personal and professional settings, and 35% of women worldwide experience physical and/or sexualized violence from a man in their lifetime (Centers for Disease Control and Prevention, 2011). So why would men be afraid of women?

I'm OK If We're OK: Men's Fears of Women in Intimate Relationships

Not only is it counter-intuitive to talk about men being afraid of women, it can be downright offensive. Why talk about men's fears of women now, in the midst of the #metoo movement? Isn't talking about men's fears of women likely to be a distraction from the very important national conversation we are trying to have about men's exploitation of women? Isn't men talking about being afraid of women like White people insisting that "all lives matter"?

As a feminist, I find it imperative that we talk about men's fears of women because these fears are one of the most powerful and pervasive shapers of men's interior lives and their relationships with women. Men's fears of women are underground, hidden from women and from themselves. Men have done such a good job of hiding their fears and vulnerabilities that even their mothers and lovers don't how scared they are.

When we stereotypically reduce our understanding of men in intimate relationships as commitment-phobic, emotionally withholding, or shut down, we do a disservice to men and profoundly misunderstand what is happening in the couple, ultimately doing a disservice to women, too. When we understand the fears that lie beneath these defensive postures in men, then everything changes.

Evidence for Men's Fears of Women

Like a conductor zipping up a piece of music, Julia gave a quick and stern "Enough," and that was it. What was so scary about her? What about that five-foot-four woman, who never inflicted physical or emotional violence, or even saw a punishment all the way through, terrified her husband and children to the point of unconditional surrender?
—Jonathan Safran Foer, *Here I Am*

Men have been afraid of women for all of recorded history. Many cultures have myths about men's inability to resist women's sexual allure, leading them to ruin—Samson and Delilah, Odysseus and the Sirens. A number of cultures have images of a vagina with teeth, *vagina dentata*, suggesting that intimacy with a woman risks emasculation. Similarly, women who are perceived as angry or aggressive are called castrating or ball busters.

The modern myth about dangerous women is the psychiatric myth of the borderline personality. Because men are not allowed to acknowledge fear of any kind, particularly fear of women, it was necessary to create a mythical category of women, so powerful as to justify men's fears. Borderline personality disorder, from the Latin, meaning "I'm scared to death of you and it's all your fault"; women who are untreatable, dangerous, for whom the only effective strategy is to erect appropriate "boundaries" to protect yourself at all cost. One of the most frightening characteristics of the borderline woman is her strong, uncensored expression of emotion, which we will discuss further in the section on "Men's fears of feeling responsible for women."

Stereotypically, we think of men being intimidated by women who earn more or are smarter than them, or being afraid of intimacy and commitment. I would like to suggest that these recognizable fears are just the tip of the iceberg. I'm going to describe six of the more important fears of women that men commonly have in intimate relationships, starting with the fears that men are likely to be more aware of and may acknowledge, and moving progressively towards fears that are largely unconscious, fears that men rarely acknowledge to themselves or others.

Men are Afraid of Being Dominated or Controlled by Women

The man is the head [of the family], but the woman is the neck.
And she can turn the head any way she wants.

—*My Big Fat Greek Wedding*

There is no more convincing evidence of men's fears of being dominated and controlled by women than their insistent protestations that they are not. Men want to see themselves as—and frequently look for ways to prove to others that they are—independent, not needing help from anybody and not influenced by others. They mock each other about having to ask their wives'/partners' permission to do anything, not wearing the pants in the family, or being a woman's bitch, projecting their own fears onto other men to reassure themselves. Notice how much of men's ridiculing of each other involves accusations about being more feminine—in other words, less masculine.

Girls are typically socialized to prepare them to run a family and a household, while boys are more often socialized to compete in the world of business and pay less attention to relationship (Joiner, 2011). It is not surprising then, that many women come into their marriages with more interest and experience in intimate relationships than their partners. Women joke with each other about needing to train their partners, about men not being a good fit off-the-rack and needing alteration.

What women want to train men on is how to be good partners for them in the social world, good fathers to their children, and good intimate partners. This can be a mutually beneficial pattern, and often goes well in couples, particularly if the woman is genuinely trying to be helpful and the man has had enough positive attachment experiences to understand that and not interpret her efforts as potential criticism.

On the other hand, the imbalance of this pattern leaves couples vulnerable to becoming polarized into rigid roles and a marriage that can feel more like a parent-child relationship than a relationship between peers. The women in these relationships often complain about the burden of running the family and the household, that their partners will "help" but never join them fully as a partner. The men in these relationships often complain about being treated like a misbehaving child, and that they are always criticized and can never get it right.

As you might expect, sexual intimacy suffers in these couples. Because the men have become more focused on avoiding conflict than achieving intimacy, sex can feel like a dangerous vulnerability. The women are often tired of being rebuffed in their approaches for emotional intimacy, which for them is a prerequisite for sexual intimacy. Hell, they can't even get him to take the garbage out! Each member of these couples is absolutely convinced that they are the victim, and that things can only get better if their partner changes, but this is a mess that they made together and the only way out is to work on it together.

Men are Afraid of Being Entrapped by Women

The preacher asked her
And she said I do
The preacher asked me

And she said yes he does too
And the preacher said
I pronounce you 99 to life
Son she's no lady she's your wife

—Lyle Lovett, "She's No Lady"

A close friend of mine went to tell his father that he planned to marry his long-term girlfriend. His father replied, "Son, marriage is an institution. If you want to spend the rest of your life in an institution, go ahead." Our cultural stereotypes paint women as eager to marry, and men as commitment-phobic; men want to remain single as long as possible and eventually accept the disadvantages of marriage in exchange for a regular sexual partner, i.e., "Why buy the cow as long as the milk is free?" In fact, the opposite is true. Marriage serves a generally protective function for men, but not for women (House, et al., 1988; Litwak, 1989; Kiecolt-Glaser, 2004). While single women are happier than single men, married women are less happy than both single women and married men (Gove, 1972). Not surprisingly then, roughly two thirds of divorces are initiated by women (Brining & Allen, 2000).

Why are men frightened of an institution that was designed to protect their property rights and overwhelmingly benefits them? In our patriarchal culture we tend to think of vulnerability and interdependence as feminine qualities. Men are socialized to be self-reliant and think of the interdependency of an intimate relationship as dangerous and potentially entrapping. In a study of projective responses to TAT (thematic apperception test) cards, men saw danger in cards depicting affiliation, whereas women saw danger in cards depicting achievement (Jordan, et al., 1991).

Men Are Afraid of Being Responsible for Women

There are two theories to arguing with a woman. Neither works.

—Will Rogers

Men worry about being responsible physically, financially and emotionally for women, in other words, for their partners' happiness. At the same time, men are also socialized to express their feelings for women by taking care of them, so that taking care of a women can also feel gratifying, more masculine. You can see how this might be confusing to their partners.

Men often feel particularly responsible for any sign of emotional distress in their partner, and instinctively react as if it is their job to "fix" that distress. I recommend a hilarious YouTube video that lampoons this pattern, "It's Not About the Nail." Men will tell you that they resent this burden, but it is largely self-imposed. Men work hard to soothe their partners' distress not just out of generosity, but often primarily to reduce the internal distress they feel whenever someone has strong feelings. Men are socialized to suppress their own emotional experience, to remain logical and calm when women are "too emotional" or "break down." Unconsciously, men understand that emotions are contagious, and that being in relationship with someone who is having strong feelings is likely to elicit stronger feelings in them as well. Men's extensive privilege in the world means that they generally experience less anxiety than women, and they would like to keep it that way. Men work hard to avoid being infected with their partners' emotional distress. Men reassuring women who are upset is similar to men buying lingerie for a woman's birthday.

This pattern of men feeling responsible for women may be mutually satisfying at first, but it tends to have a short shelf life. While women are initially willing to accept caretaking as an expression of love, most women eventually want a more mutually intimate relationship. Over time, women become less appreciative of their partner's caretaking, and then men become more resentful about not being appreciated. From the men's perspective, they've been kind, considerate, and helpful; in short, they've done everything that could be asked of them. So, what in the world have they failed at now?

Men Are Afraid of Being Exposed as Inadequate with Women

If you really need me,
Just reach out and touch me.
Come on honey, tell me so.

—Rod Stewart, "Da Ya Think I'm Sexy"

Men are socialized to equate masculinity with self-confidence, to put up a good front and always present as self-assured, even when they are not; "Never let them see you sweat." Accordingly, men's fears of being inadequate go underground, hidden from themselves and from other men. Men are afraid of being exposed as emotionally and sexually inadequate in their intimate relationships with women.

On some level, men often recognize that they are not as emotionally well developed as their wives/partners. Their wives/partners seem to have stronger emotions, an easier time expressing their feelings, and more empathy in response to other people's feelings. On a deeply unconscious level, men are often scared that there is something wrong with them when they don't have the kinds of emotional responses they see in their wives/partners. Interestingly, Freud theorized that when little girls saw their brother's or father's penis, they would feel inadequate, but said nothing about little boys seeing their mother's or sister's open expression of emotion and feeling inadequate about that.

Men are also deeply afraid of being exposed as sexually inadequate in their intimate relationships with women. There is an old saying that women need to feel loved to want to have sex, and that men need to have sex to feel loved. While men are stereotypically portrayed as self-centered and compartmentalized lovers (Diamond, 2017), research suggests that pleasing their partner is often more important to men than their own pleasure. This paradox is readily resolved when we understand that men's focus on their partners' pleasure is only partially an act of generosity, and often an effort to stave off their own feelings of insecurity.

Approaching a woman openly with their sexual desires is an inherently vulnerable act for men that often stirs up deep-seated fears of inadequacy. Women are often surprised at the strength of their husband/partner's emotional response when turned down for sex, mistakenly attributing those reactions to misguided notions about the strength of male libido. Similarly, women often misunderstand men's wish that they initiate sex more often as a simple request for more sex. When women are more open about their own sexual desires, it frees men from the insecurity they often feel about being rejected, or more profoundly, from feeling not desirable or even not lovable. Men often feel like they are putting their entire sense of worth on the line when they approach their partners sexually. Intercourse for men is a literal return to the insides of a woman's body, the place from whence they came, so it is a powerfully regressive experience, the ultimate reassurance of their acceptance and symbolically a powerful test of their self-worth.

Men Are Afraid of Being Abandoned

Men act so tough and strong on the outside because on the inside, we are scared, weak, and fragile. Men, not women, are the weaker sex.

—Jerry Rubin

Here I begin talking about fears that are largely unconscious, fears that underlie the previously described more conscious fears. One of the most profound and deeply buried fears for many men is that their inadequacies will eventually lead to their partners abandoning them, and that they will not be able to take care of themselves. In the classic "still face experiment" (Tronick, 1975), a mother is instructed to continue looking at her infant child but to adopt a "still face," that is, to stop responding emotionally to her child in any way. The infant becomes visibly distressed in a shockingly brief period. Because men generally do not have very well developed intimate relationships outside of marriage (Joiner, 2011), they are often surprisingly emotionally dependent on their partners for reassurance that they will not be abandoned, showing visible distress when their partners do not reassure them by listening attentively, providing a home for them, and being sexually interested and available.

As a result, conflict with their partner is extremely threatening to many men. Some men become so conflict avoidant that emotional withdrawal becomes their primary coping strategy. They focus primarily on avoiding their wives'/partners' disapproval and criticism, and largely abandon any efforts to talk about their own needs or work towards getting closer to their partners. Women often get frustrated or angry at their husbands'/partners' withdrawal and push harder for the closeness and connection they want. Since men are socialized to feel responsible for any unhappiness in their partners, they often hear their partner's request for more intimacy as a complaint, or even an indictment for doing something wrong or lacking in some important way. They react to what they hear as criticism by being defensive, frustrating their partners further by creating even more distance. These couples are often locked in a mutually escalating destructive cycle, feeling equally lost and helpless about how to find their way out.

Femiphobia

Freud says, Man fears that his strength will be taken from him by woman, dreads becoming infected by her femininity and proving himself a weakling. Masculinity must fight off effeminacy day by day. Woman and nature stand ever ready to reduce the male to boy and infant.

—Camille Paglia

Femiphobia, a term coined by psychologist Stephen Ducat (2004), is both a fear of being thought of by others as feminine and an underlying fear of aspects of the self that are more stereotypically associated with the feminine, such as emotions, vulnerability and yearning for emotional intimacy. Femiphobia is the core fear underlying all of the above fears. What overtly appears to be a fear of women is actually a fear of being feminized. Femiphobia is the fear that underlies misogyny.

Boys become men through a process of separation from their initial identification with their mothers. Consequently, we have tended to define masculinity more as what it is not, i.e. feminine, than what it is. Noted sex therapist Esther Perel talks about what she calls the fragility of the male identity. "When we make a girl play with a truck, we don't think it's going to make her less of a girl. But, when we think of a boy playing with a doll, we think it's going to weaken his essence as a man" (Marikar, 2018).

Many cultures have rituals for boys' initiation into manhood. In non-industrialized cultures, those rituals often involve a group of men coming in the middle of the night to kidnap the initiate from the women's hut where he has been living with his mother and the other women,

The young man is taken into the wilderness for a series of rituals and trials, at the end of which he is considered by his community to be a man. In one such story, when the young man returns to his village, his mother comes out to greet him, and he slaps her in the face before gathering his belongings and moving into the men's hut. The ritual is initiated with a symbolic kidnapping in recognition of the fact that the young man might be reluctant to give up all the emotional comforts and intimacy of the world of women, even in exchange for the power and privilege of joining the world of men. Similarly, the young man slaps his mother when he returns because otherwise he might run crying into her arms and beg her to take him back.

Clinical Application

My early training was in phenomenological psychology, which taught me a particular approach to listening to people's experience. As I have listened to the men in my practice talk about their relationships over many years, it gradually began to dawn on me that they were scared of their partners. At first, that seemed like an outlandish, if not disrespectful, idea, so I kept it to myself. However, I kept hearing it again and again, until I became increasingly convinced that the majority, if not all, of the straight men I was working with were scared of their partners. Everything I've written in this article is simply a retelling of the stories that men have told me in my office.

My first forays into exploring this idea came with simply using the word "scared" in conversation with men. I chose that word because I anticipated that its bluntness would best help men connect with the feeling. Almost to a man, when I suggested that they might be scared of their partner, men momentarily bowed up, preparing to defend themselves, and then before they even had a chance to mount much of a denial, a look of recognition and understanding slowly dawned on their faces. While I certainly do not endorse the idea that the number of patients in one's practice is some measure of therapeutic acumen, I don't think it's a coincidence that since I've started working with these ideas my practice has gone from being primarily women (as is typically the case) to a practice that is about two-thirds male.

Let me give you a clinical scenario I think will be familiar to many of you, and then show you how that situation looks when understood through the lens of men's fears of

I'm OK If We're OK: Men's Fears of Women in Intimate Relationships

women. A man and woman in a committed relationship have an argument. The woman is visibly hurt and angry, while the man remains fairly stoic, and nonresponsive. The woman experiences the man's nonresponsiveness as a painful withdrawal. The more he withdraws, the stronger her feelings become and the more she pursues him, trying to connect emotionally with him. The stronger the woman's feelings become, the more the man withdraws. They are locked in a mutually escalating destructive cycle.

Ten years ago, I might have understood this man's emotional withholding as a way to maintain power and control in the relationship. While I still think there is some truth in that, today I would primarily understand it as a man who is scared of what he feels when his wife is more emotional. He is aware that his partner is upset, and her tears make him surprisingly uncomfortable. While he would like to feel empathic, there is something about her strong feelings that is distressing to him and gets in the way. He withdraws primarily to protect himself from his own feelings, and from his fears that there is something wrong with him, that he is lacking basic compassion and human responsiveness.

I think a more in-depth understanding of the man's part of this relational impasse can help him connect with a broader range of emotional experience. This will also be more satisfying to his partner and help her move to a more understanding and compassionate place.

References:

Brining, M.F., & Allen, D.W. (2000). 'These boots are made for walking': Why most divorce filers are women. *American Law and Economics Review*, 2, (1),126-169

Centers for Disease Control and Prevention (2011). Infographic based on data from the National Intimate Partner and Sexual Violence Survey (NISVS): 2010-2012 state report. https: www.cdc.gov/violenceeprevention/pdf/NISVS-inforgraphic-2016.pdf

Diamond, J. (2017). The one thing men want more than sex. https://goodmenproject.com/sex-relationships/the-one-thing-men-want-more-than-sex-wcz/

Ducat, S. (2004) *The wimp factor: Gender gaps, holy wars, and the politics of anxious masculinity*. Boston: Beacon Press.

Gove, W.R. (1972). The relationship between sex roles, marital status and mental illness. *Social Forces*, 51, 4-44.

Headley, J. (2013). It's not about the nail. https://www.youtube.com/watch?v=-4EDhdAHrOg&feature=youtube

House, J.S., Landis, K.R. & Umberson, D. (1988). Social relationships and health. *Science*, 241, 540-545

Joiner, T. (2011). *Lonely at the top: The high cost of men's success*. New York: St. Martin's Press.

Jordan, J., Kaplan, A., Stiver, I., Surrey, J and Baker Miller, J. (1991). *Women's growth in connection: Writings from the Stone Center*. New York: Guilford.

Kiecolt-Glaser, J.K., & Newton, T.L. Marriage and health: his and hers. *Psychological Bulletin*, 127, 472-503.

Litwak, E., Messeri, P., Wolfe, S., Gorman, S., Silverstein, M. & Guilarte, M. (1989). Organization theory, social supports and mortality rates: A theoretical convergence. *American Sociological Review*, 54, 49-66

Marikar, S. (2018). Teachable moment: He said, she said. *New Yorker*, March 26. P. 21

Tronick, E., Adamson, L.B., Als, H., & Brazelton, T.B. (1975, April). Infant emotions in normal and perturbated interactions. Paper presented at the biennial meeting of the Society for Research in Child Development, Denver, CO.

Mitchell Foy

A part of me
missing
comes forward
cloaked in the guise
of you

Elizabeth E. Field

ELIZABETH E. FIELD, MA, LMFT, LCAS, earned her undergraduate degree in psychology, minoring in philosophy and religion, from ASU in 1996. She obtained her graduate education at ASU in marriage and family therapy in 1999. Since her graduating year she has attended AAP as her primary continuing education training. She has practiced psychotherapy since 1998. Currently she has a full-time private practice in Charlotte, North Carolina. Her most recent interests are sex therapy and couple's therapy. For her, these areas are an opportunity to bridge her previous work in addiction and trauma with the art of healing by creating healthy relationships. She is married and has two sons (12 and 4 years old) and a yellow lab-mix dog who inspire her daily.
clt.therapy.elizabethfield@gmail.com

Interview with Ellen Fox

Editor's note: This interview was lightly edited for clarity.

Elizabeth Field: What do you think it says that you are a sex therapist housed in God's house?

Ellen Fox: I hope it indicates that sexuality is blessed by God—that sexuality is a healthy part of life, of marriage, and of who we are, created by God, in His essence and function. Let me tell you about my earliest connection with my church-employer. I was asked to speak at a Valentine's Day dinner entitled, "Creating a More Intimate Marriage." I thought, well, this may stop all my referrals from the church! I am glad to say that it was well received. Afterwards, people gathered around and asked me lots of questions about marital sexuality. It wasn't too long after that I was offered my job—with a luxurious office! So, I think this reveals that many believers are open to conversations about faith and sex.

Field: There is potential for silence around what people of faith are taught or think about sexuality. How do you handle the mythology of sex or distortions of sexuality?

Fox: I explore some of that with people in session, and I invite them to explore their beliefs, myths, or narratives about sex as part of a sexual development history, a set of questions aimed at helping couples openly talk about their individual and couple sexuality. It can really be odd to be asked about your sexual myths. Most people would say, "All my sexual ideas are healthy, reasonable and understandable." I listen for sexual myths and point them out when I hear them—and there are lots of denigrating

Ellen Fox

sexual myths about men and women, including how we're supposed to experience arousal and desire. I want to help couples have sex that includes spontaneity, creativity and fun, and I think that is godly because it deeply connects them. This can be an uncomfortable thought for some—even bad to some people—and the concept that sex is bad can hinder couples from enjoying intimacy.

Field: Maybe that constraint applies to therapists as well as their patients. I think psychotherapists shy away from spirituality, theology, or God and sexuality in psychotherapy unless they have special training.

Fox: I agree with you, Elizabeth. I don't think clients bring their sexual concerns to us unless they feel safe to, or have some sort of an invitation from us. I think perhaps their silence parallels ours—and sometimes, our silence parallels theirs.

Field: I think we can weave these three together—silence, sex and spirituality.

Fox: I agree. In regard to spirituality, God's creation of sex is a picture of God's love—being known and deeply loved, and invited to love. God created sex for procreation, but also as a means of us being safely known and loved by another, in a committed relationship. I think our silence can have several different meanings—it could reveal our respect for God's sacred gift of sex, or it could suggest shame about our sexual self that we don't identify, or voice. Another place where I notice silence is when parents attempt to teach their children about sexuality, including healthy boundaries and modesty. These parental tasks aren't meant to promote silence, but to protect

ELLEN FOX is a licensed marriage and family therapist and a certified sex therapist with the American Board of Christian Sex Therapists, and she is on staff at Western Avenue Baptist Church, Statesville, North Carolina, where she provides marital, family, and individual psychotherapy to persons throughout the life span. She received a MAEd in counseling from Wake Forest University, and a PhD in marriage and family therapy from Northcentral University, Prescott Valley, Arizona. She has been married to her best friend, Clark, for 42 years, and has two married adult children and six grandchildren, who are all the loves of her life. She finds incredible joy in her relationship with God, providing therapy, and playing her 1968 John Sipe violin.
ellen@westernavenue.org

the child and their sexual self. My hope as an LMFT and a certified sex therapist is to promote respect, not shame, for God's gift of sex.

Field: Can you talk more about how you handle shame as it relates to sexuality?

Fox: Sexual shame can enter therapy spoken and unspoken, from a number of different places. For example, family-of-origin silence regarding sexuality, with limited—or absent—conversations about healthy sexual maturation, could have implied that sex was dirty or shameful, thus negatively impacting a couple's sexual openness. Others might feel shame because they think they sinned against God by being sexual outside of God's guidelines. Sexual shame is often associated with a history of sexual abuse or trauma, including exposure to sexually explicit information before developmental maturation. So while individuals may not address shame initially upon beginning therapy, I invite them to a conversation about sexual "brakes or accelerators," or constraints to healthy sexual functioning.

If their shame is from sexual trauma, I may refer for EMDR to aid in healing. I see positive outcomes with EFT [emotionally focused therapy], and I work toward strengthening marital attachment, with the outcome of greater sexual intimacy. My goal is for individuals' shame to be identified, processed, and ultimately healed, so that they can have the satisfying sexual relationship they desire. And I believe that the ultimate healing from shame is God-created. While we don't know what to do with shameful feelings about sex, I believe that God does. He gets it and understands our pain. He made us, so He knows us and our sexual self—our desire, arousal, conception and orgasm. We bear our shame silently, but He understands us and our pain—and I believe He wants to heal us from our shame.

Field: Is this what you refer to in your book as "Godly care of shame"?

Fox: Yes, that is one way. Ultimately where I am going with this is whether they believe forgiveness is possible, and whether they feel that God can forgive them. I help them explore that because I fully believe that we can be forgiven—that God can love us no more or less. He desires to forgive us and to have a loving and open relationship with us—which is a beautiful picture of what a healthy marriage is—where we can be open and deeply loved, and where we experience grace, not shame.

Field: So, marriage can be a place of wholly loving another person?

Fox: Oh, yes! In essence, where they see themselves as naked and unashamed with their mate—worthy of, and wholly loved by, their spouse. Because that is ultimately where I am hoping to go—feeling loved and accepted by their mate, and loved by God.

Field: So, in that way they are offered the choice to decide their brakes or accelerators not based on shame but on what feels good, comfortable, or is what they want?

Fox: Yes, I attempt to help couples sort this out. Part of the conversation in sex therapy focuses on each partner's view of what are the sexual brakes or accelerators in their relationship, while I listen closely for indicators of shame. Couples are offering one another the gift of themselves, created in God's image. I use the words "Godly eroticism" because marital sexual intimacy is definitely acceptable in the eyes of God! For example, a couple's differing desire for sexual frequency, or behaviors, may not be shame-based, but may be about their own likes/dislikes, circadian rhythm, stress level, unresolved marital conflict, or personal narratives about sexual assertiveness or receptivity.

Field: Right, isn't that what you referred to as the great secret of sex in "A Celebration of Sex"?

Fox: Yes, people struggle to say the word "God" and "sex" in the same sentence, or even in the same room, yet a deep marital friendship between two people who have an authentic faith in God helps promote a good sex life. And really, God knows everything, so don't you think He knows all about your sexual relationship? This sounds adolescent, but He created sex, for us.

Field: You are saying sex is a metaphor for who God is?

Fox: Yes, a loving metaphor into who our God is—all knowing, all loving, and wanting us to know Him. Yet sex is an actual event—a moment—when you can experience being deeply loved by someone else. A profound kind of loving because in that moment you are allowing someone to be in charge of your body, and you are giving them permission to provide you pleasure.

Field: That is exciting.

Fox: Yes, even the thought of it is arousing! It is the loving binding of mind, body, and heart that so connects. Which is why I find the idea of sex as a hobby, or having multiple partners, doesn't make sense.

Field: Can you talk about God's guidelines or God's economy?

Fox: Yes, I can. I see people of different faiths and many who do not have a professed faith. But because I practice out of a church, I often ask people if a Christian "lens" is part of what they want. They may say "not necessarily," so I say, "ok, I appreciate you letting me know that. I can move that aside, but it is part of how I see the human condition, who we are, and treatment—will that be ok with you?" Couples have shared that even though they didn't have a specific faith, they thought my faith would include good values, a moral "fence around the yard," you could say. So, my quickest answer to the question is that God's sexual guidelines fit into Judeo-Christian principles, especially promoting marital sexuality and monogamy.

Field: So, there can be a lot of pressure on our sex life?

Fox: Oh yes, in our sexually-saturated culture, there can be. Like a couple who wants to conceive, yet they have struggled with sexual performance issues—whether problems with ejaculation, or dyspareunia. Or desire to be orgasmic and an inability to be. Or health concerns that negatively impact their sexual relationship. I spend a lot of time helping couples realize that intimacy is much more than a set of sexual behaviors. I spend a lot of time normalizing: This is where you are at this time in your life. I help them work toward intimacy, even though they may not be achieving the sexual outcome they're hoping for.

Field: Can you talk about the paradox of maturity and childlike qualities involved in sexual relationships?

Fox: As if maturity does not include fun, curiosity, a desire to know and a sense of awe! I think maturity is about putting off immediate gratification for long-term gain. I think sexual intimacy includes a "godly selflessness" and a "godly selfishness," where at times you focus on your partner, and at times you focus on your own sexual pleasure—and this takes individual, and couple, maturity.

Field: What do you think about marriage in the 21st century? Do you think sex is a cure for the marriage dilemma?

Fox: Well, I always get tickled when I ask how things are going and my patients say, "Everything is great. We have had sex!" We laugh, and I tell them, "Get out of here!" I just love when my couples reach their goals! Because sex releases oxytocin, it can really strengthen attachment to our mate. I also like to remind my couples in their 80s and 90s who can no longer have intercourse that they can still be deeply intimate with each other.

And while I read that the divorce rate has dropped slightly, I fear that people stay in unsatisfying marriages. My bias is that I don't want people to be in an intact but unsatisfying marriage. I grieve for them when their marriages are not satisfying, and I feel we have a lot of work as a profession to help people feel more satisfied in their marriages.

Field: What do you think helps people feel more satisfied in marriage?

Fox: I am looking for what we can do to have more positives than negatives, help them feel safe to remain open and vulnerable, help them maintain and deepen their emotional connection, and face what is there and not pretend it is not there. To be "naked and unashamed," which is how it loops back to sexuality to me. That is what I am working toward.

Field: How do you think about sexual wholeness and spiritual wholeness?

Fox: I think we are in a lifelong process of becoming whole, spiritually whole. I say, "Staying close to the vine," connected to our God who loves us. Our part is staying connected to God through faith, whether that is connection to Him through His word, meditation, staying connected to other believers, or prayer.

There are people of no faith who have satisfying sexual relationships. My bias is that a deeply spiritual relationship promotes a deeply satisfying sexual relationship. Knowing we are so loved and can be loved no more by the Creator of the universe I think emboldens us to love another person! I also have seen amazing individuals who report having no faith, and they experience a deeply satisfying sexual relationship. And I consider being sexual healthy as a sense of ownership, not shameful.

Field: How do you promote sexual health?

Fox: I promote sexual health mainly through marital fidelity and commitment, and to parents of children, helping them have conversations regarding their child's sexuality. This includes appreciating their masculinity or femininity, and their value as a human being created by God. I work toward helping parents normalize sexual maturation and development, while protecting children and helping them understand healthy boundaries. I try to loop it back to our value of who they are as a person—that their sexual self is a part of who God created them to be.

Field: What do you think our culture is missing with its movement toward "anything goes, there are no limits," as you stated with the fence analogy?

Fox: I fear culture has become insatiable and says "the next best thing is still out there." So, there is no moment to be mindful, to be present, and just be enveloped in the arms of your loved one and to love them dearly. And when there are no limits, there is a selfish belief that everything is for me. So, instead of resting safely in the arms of the one who loves you, in the ability to know and be known by this person, it says something else is better, so don't be satisfied. Don't be satisfied with what you have and what is available right now and here in this moment because satisfaction is always out there.

It also set up the tendency to be a spectator in the sexual relationship, which makes it hard to experience pleasure or be orgasmic. It is hard to be mindful and focused on the building of arousal when there is something else better. What sexual pleasure is also about is being in the moment. Being present.

Field: So that takes me back to God, presence, being mindful, being in the moment, aware.

Fox: Yes, I agree with you. That we are choosing to be present with another human being who is flawed, another person fearfully and wonderfully made and loved by God—like me. We are really gifted with the privilege of being with them as well, and so there is a sense of mutual gratitude. And I hope lots of excitement and a lot of arousal! They offer you the gift of themselves. Treasure isn't enough of a word.

Field: Awesome.

Fox: And yet all we have to do is look at magazines covers that say something like, "100 ways to improve your sex life." Then next month, "Here are another 100 ways to improve your sex life." I think it discounts and denigrates the privilege of being with another person.

So, when couples desire novelty, and this is ok, I loop it back around to this couple and say, "Look at your spouse's face right now. Does their expression look like they feel

Interview with Ellen Fox   **39**

deeply loved? Cherished?" That is a very important moment. I am thinking, is this behavior likely to cause this couple to feel closer and deeply attached? And so I ask them, "Do you feel deeply loved and cherished as your mate describes this?" If not, I help them unpack that. Is that prior memories or a negative connotation? Is it just a no thank you, I don't want that, and your mate can't hear that? What is it?

Field: So, that is your indicator, are they moving toward or away from each other?

Fox: Yes, sometimes as a sex therapist people may think I have a list of acceptable or unacceptable behaviors, but rarely is that the case. Sex therapy can certainly be about specific behaviors, but it is often more a question of what hinders this couple from experiencing joyous intimacy.

Field: What do you think therapists miss by leaving out the sexual piece?

Fox: I would tell them, jump in, seek education and supervision, and see how wonderful it is to help couples with this part of their relationship! I would say if you are open to working with sexuality at all, then do some continuing education. Part of what will happen to you is a very systematic desensitization, so you'll have a language and you'll learn what to do with all the feelings you have inside. I would ask therapists to be open to learning, and they'll gain skills which help them become accustomed to the not knowing.

Field: What would you say to therapists who leave God out of the sexual equation?

Fox: Well, I am aware there are just different ways to provide therapy, even though I think that as a whole, the majority of therapists are open to clients' varied beliefs and faiths. So, I would invite them to consider making even more room for the spiritual in session. I find that marital sexuality is deeply spiritual, and I would invite psychotherapists to consider it.

Sexuality and Spirituality:
One Man's Journey

John Rhead

JOHN RHEAD, PhD, was born in Utah, raised in Colorado, educated in New Hampshire and California, and finally settled in Maryland. His first job out of school involved doing research with LSD. He worked in a prison, a private psychiatric hospital, an educational center for disturbed youth, and a medical school before settling down into private practice. He is grateful for many people and many things in his life.
jrheadphd@gmail.com

WHEN I WAS IN MY TEENS, A SONG ENTITLED "NEVER ON SUNDAY" WAS POPULAR. The singer addresses a man, saying that he could kiss her anytime Monday through Saturday, but not on Sunday because that was her "day of rest." It was one of three occasions that Mom gave me some sex education. She got angry (very unusual for her) at the way the song seemed to imply that God did not approve of sex (Sunday = Sabbath in our Mormon home, even though Mom was not a Mormon), and that sex was a burden or a chore, rather than a pleasure, for women. Only yesterday, almost 60 years later, did it occur to me that she was also angry about the sexist implication that men could enjoy sex but women could not.

Mom was also the launching pad for my spiritual journey. She grew up on a farm in rural Indiana and attended a small Christian church at the crossroads, but her hunger for spiritual knowledge and experience was not suppressed by these circumstances. She read widely about religion and spirituality, so there were always books around the house, like *A Testament of Devotion* (Kelly, 1996) that invited me to explore such intriguing areas.

My father's messages about sexuality were few and almost uniformly negative. The gist of it was that sex was dangerous, and especially so outside of marriage. When he learned that I had moved in with my girlfriend during graduate school, he launched into a tirade. I let him rant for quite a while and then impatiently interrupted him: "Oh, come on, Dad. You know that you and your friends were doing the same thing when you were my age!" His instant response: "Of course we did! But we had the decency to feel guilty!"

When I was feeling atheistic (with some thoughts of suicide) in a part of my teens, Dad argued the logic of believing in God. It might make me feel better and, if I found out when I died that I was mistaken, at least the illusion would have made my life a little more tolerable. In the final decades of his life, the only thing I remember hearing from him was, "If God exists, He's a son of a bitch and I hate Him."

I wonder now how I have woven these early lessons from my parents into my current views of sexuality and spirituality.

I was delighted when I heard about Tantric sex in my early 20s. I remember being thrilled and relieved that somebody saw the two as related. The bit of sexual experience I had by then led me to believe that something very powerful was involved that was difficult to attribute merely to a reproductive instinct. What I experienced on those (rare) occasions when I did have sex was that I wanted to experience something more with the woman I was with. This happened with one-night stands and even once with a prostitute. I remember being teased by my college classmates for how much I actually seemed to want to talk with women as well as seduce them.

I began to distinguish between *having sex* and *making love*. Making love seemed to be something deeper and more powerful than having sex. This became very clear when my girlfriend and I used smoking a joint as our foreplay. We were sometimes so synchronized in our passion that a kind of merger seemed to take place, and as we moved toward simultaneous orgasms (or perhaps toward sharing a single huge orgasm), I felt I might be annihilated by the power of it. I made a conscious decision to surrender to this power, even if it meant that I would die in the process.

It is the notion of surrender that first bridged sexuality and spirituality for me. I had certainly read many reports by mystics of various types (thanks, Mom) who talked about surrendering to something larger and more powerful than themselves. Such surrenders seemed usually to involve experiences of ecstasy, which I could certainly relate to my own sexual experiences.

Although I am sure I had some mystical experiences of my own before discovering psychedelics, when I read about (and later experienced directly) what these substances could facilitate, I knew I was onto something. Although a very good connection with a skilled guide is necessary to ensure safety and maximize the possibility of a transcendent experience, it still amazes me that we can fairly reliably attain such states using these substances (sometimes quite appropriately referred to as sacraments). Perhaps even more amazing is the way in which, once experienced, these states can be more easily accessed even without the assistance of a psychedelic.

So it is with what might be called *sacred sexuality*. Once it has been experienced, with or without chemical assistance, one knows that it exists as a possibility and one can intentionally pursue it with one's lover. Sometimes when I am working with a couple who are trying to "improve" their sexual relationship, usually in terms of frequency of having sex, I give them a warning. I tell them that if they are not careful they may find that having sex will lead them to making love. Often I say this in a playful or joking manner, but I mean it when I say it. What I have never said, since it only recently occurred to me, is that couples may avoid sex for precisely that reason. They may intuit in some unconscious way that having sex can open up something deeper and more powerful that they may not feel quite ready to surrender to.

The explicitly spiritual version of such a fear was presented to me by a woman I saw many years ago. She was a devout spiritual seeker and regular meditator. Her husband, with whom she had an active and intense sexual relationship, was a medical researcher who was objective and scientific in his approach to the world. One day she persuaded him to join her in a meditative practice that she had found powerful. He did so, and to her (and his!) amazement, he had a profound experience of mystical rapture. It terrified him so much that he refused to ever try anything like meditation again, and moved toward spending more time in his research laboratory and less time in the bedroom with her. Eventually she left him.

These days I sometimes tell client couples (and remind myself) that there are basically two reasons other than making a baby to have sex: (1) because one or both parties are in the mood, and (2) because it is good for the relationship. Sometimes I compare it to regular physical exercise, like running or biking. Most of the time it should be enjoyable, but sometimes you do it just because it is good for you.

What I have not yet shared with a client couple is my growing belief that making love is good for the planet. This seems especially likely to be true if there is some ritual as part of the foreplay. Lighting a candle and setting an intention (or saying a prayer) that the lovemaking will actually make (i.e., make manifest) love, and that this love will radiate out to the world, would seem to enhance the potential impact on the planet. Similarly, remaining in a gentle silent embrace for an extended period of time after the orgasm(s), would seem to provide not only an opportunity for the couple's intimacy to deepen, but also for whatever love has been created to radiate out to the rest of the world.

I wonder if writing this down will give me the courage to start saying such things to clients.   ▼

References

Kelly, T. R. (1996), *A testament of devotion*. San Francisco: Harper Books.

Norcross, J. C., & Lambert, M. J. (2011). Psychotherapy relationships that work II. *Psychotherapy, 48*(1), 4-8.

Bruce Knight

Bruce Wayne Knight, LMFT, LPCA, CSAT, CST, MDiv, MAMFT, is a marriage and family therapist specializing in comprehensive sex addiction recovery, sex therapy, attachment repair, and spiritual formation. Having experienced his own recovery journey, 6 years of pastoring, 33 years of group facilitation, and therapy trainings, he works with addicts, partners, and groups to provide comprehensive treatment. Bruce is married to Kitty Knight. They are parents of two awesome, successful daughters, Erin Knight and Laura Knight-Bebee.
brucewknight1@gmail.com

Befriending Silence in Therapy

How do I experience silence? Let me count the ways.

There is that moment of silence that comes before the storm of shock, anger, bargaining, depression, and acceptance when first we realize that something valuable to us has died. There is that deadening, chilling silence that comes when the couple has reached that familiar state of impasse and has nothing more to say. There are those moments of focused centering, emotional regulating, and physiological calming silence in beginning my men's group when we prepare ourselves to fully receive group's benefits. There are those moments of intentional solitude with God, when we experience simultaneously the awe of his majestic presence and an intimacy as close as our own breath. There is the terrifying silence that comes when a client feels overwhelmed, sinking in the shame of his relationship-destructive behavior, and fights back a watershed of tears. There is the silence of the avoidant attachment style client who never learned to feel or deal with his emotions.

There are many forms, experiences, and occasions for silence, welcomed or unwelcomed. We may have missed the benefits of silence by surrounding ourselves with white noise or becoming too dependent on modern technology to notice. We have missed probably hundreds of thousands of moments of peace, insight, connecting, and truly healthy power by veering away from silence! One thing is absolutely true: Silence is an integral part of our humanity and as such, for a therapist, it is vital to become friends with it.

Personal Moments of Unwanted Silence in Session

When I have been tracking with my client, immersing myself into his story, her pain, their aloneness, and his shame, all of a sudden I find myself stymied by internal silence. Pause! In the midst of my work, I may float in and out of a task-oriented model, working with the client to establish a baseline sobriety, then shift my focus to potential attachment wounds as they present themselves in the course of the session, and then I may also transition to a significant point of spirituality before fully coming back to the client. Nonetheless, that internal silence can be very disquieting to me in the midst of a therapy session. I have found myself lost in their journey or in parallel thoughts momentarily. At times, I feel mentally bogged down and guilty for not providing the client a full session. In healthier moments afterwards I am reminded that this experience is part of being human. My performance expectations recede to reasonable levels. I take a number of deep cleansing breaths, center myself in my ongoing relationship with God, and utilize a sentence prayer I created years ago. "I am yours, you are mine." Then, I continue with daily responsibilities. I repeat this prayer numerous times throughout the day.

The Isolating Silence of Shame

Often, this silence is evident from the time the client walks into our office. Posture, head positioning, eye contact, gestures, and tone and cadence of speech unveil it. During the course of the first session's preliminaries, I observe the silent messages. Usually clients begin, "I have sexual issues," or, "My spouse says I have a problem." I watch for the telltale signs of silent shame.

As a certified sex addiction therapist tapping into my own recovery journey, I am equipped to more effectively enter my client's internal experience. I continue to develop a healthy partnership with silent shame experienced in self and clients so that I hear the healing message underneath the isolating and demeaning one. Unhealthy shame draws attention to debilitating self-talk. "I am broken, warped, worthless, a pervert!" I create therapeutic experiences to enable these addicts to identify that shame and their underlying needs. Addressing this shame begins before a first session with overt and covert messages of acceptance. From the time the client makes the first contact, spoken words of affirmation in calm, comforting tones are offered. Comforting written words flow through emails. Clients are greeted in our center with soothing visual art, nervous system-calming tiered water fountains, and diffused relaxing essential oils. Clients' ears are treated to relaxing and mentally stimulating music.

The male clients I see range in severity from sexual behavior impairing themselves and relationships to sex and porn addiction destroying marriages, damaging careers, and depleting finances. Typically, in a first session, although verbally silent, the client's body language speaks volumes. He is fidgety, restless, uncomfortable, and sits with hands folded as if in a position of hiding. I begin each session with verbal, facial, and tonal assurances indicating this is a safe place of acceptance and I will honor his autonomy as the driver of each session. I also reassure him by normalizing his journey with the many others and myself who have been on it. "You are not alone."

What I have gleaned from all the dead ends, the relapses, and the dangling needs of my spouse without appropriate help in our recovery journey is a deeper level of insight into the pain and shame of clients. Those benefits continue to inform connection and attachment repair with my internally isolated addicts.

After conveying those assurances, I turn the session over to the client to hear what brought him to me. His pre-existing anxiety begins to escalate. He may begin at discovery. After years of a silent double life, hiding behaviors out of fear of rejection or abandonment, shame or guilt, his spouse discovers an email, a text, pornographic history, or escort sites. If he has been wrestling with his addiction, he may begin from his earliest sexual memories, experience of abuse, and exposure to porn, or other entry points for coping that became compulsive.

Customarily, there are anxious facial expressions, eyes cast downward, or hand wringing. As I listen with rapt attunement, validation, conveying empathy, and matching the level of my emotion with his, a gradual relief begins to occur. If his shame begins to reach an intolerable point, I may bring that to the present, attune with his experience of the emotion, and depathologize his coping as impaired ways of attempting to meet legitimate attachment needs or cope with intolerable abuse. As he shares his story and experiences acceptance, validation, and empathy, silent shame is distilled into more beneficial information. His nervous system begins to quiet, and his dysregulated emotional state begins to be co-regulated. In the silence of his isolating shame, he has experienced comfort, acceptance, and freedom from judgment. This instills safety, security, and hope.

The silencing power of shame may continue for a long while in recovery. It is very common in a 3- to 5-year recovery journey that individuals will experience relapse. Lack of awareness tends to be the most consistent problem. The silent "killers" are the times of stress in which awareness of impaired thinking, emotional dysregulation, and relational distance are not addressed. These dynamics leave people vulnerable. Coupled with insufficient positive accountability, relapse is guaranteed.

The depth of silent shame's grip is seen in individuals who have experienced acceptance and still struggle with keeping secrets until they relapse. Once they begin to disclose secrets, they discover again that they are accepted and valued and have their worth validated as inherent, not performance based. We have found that one silent thief of personal congruence is a life valued for its performance rather than its existence. As clients integrate inherent worth into their lives, they become more congruent with whom they are and experience healing.

The Silence of Distorted Intimacy

The silence of distorted intimacy is closely affiliated to the shame, because it interrupts one's ability to initiate and maintain healthy intimacy on at least three levels: emotion, sexuality, and spirituality. It is a silent, dormant, and unrecognized issue. It is an impaired internal working model of relationship that displays itself in dysfunctional and ineffective attempts at connecting and comfort seeking. My clients' experiences confirm that all three areas of intimacy are interwoven. Because of this, I find myself working persistently toward integrating four components: sex addiction recovery, attachment repair, spiritual formation, and restoration of healthy sexuality.

As I begin to conduct love/attachment style assessments and family-of-origin interviews and learn more about my clients' coping styles, each displays similar themes. In early childhood they experienced insecure attachment. Many experienced emotional, physical, sexual, or spiritual abuse. Although they may not have experienced big-T Trauma, they experienced relational trauma with the same outcomes: children who became disconnected and avoidant or preoccupied and anxious.

As this silence of distorted intimacy continues, it displays itself in clients who conflate sexuality and connectedness, confusing a fundamental distinction. An example of this occurred during a group session on healthy sexuality. I floated the statement, "At some point each of you will get to the place where you can look at a scantily clothed woman and appreciate her God-given beauty without objectifying." One guy looked dumbfounded! The obvious perplexity in his mind was, how could that ever be? At the foundation of this client's perspective is the silence concerning sexuality and intimacy these clients experienced in their childhood homes. A sexuality survey that I conduct asks the question, "How did you learn about sex?" The predominant answer given is on their own, or from peers. Without impugning parents, we accurately identify where the client is to help him grow. In many homes, the issue of sex remains silent, and skewed notions and practices ensue. We work toward discovery of these notions, expectations, and confusion underlying the silence. After gaining sobriety, we help them integrate a healthy view of sexuality.

Another type of distorted intimacy we see is distorted spirituality. A number of clients have experienced spiritual abuse in childhood. A pastor's son, whose father was relocated by the denomination as a way of handling his affairs, learned to remain silent about the affairs and all of his emotions. This particular client is working toward forgiveness, relinquishing resentment, and sobriety and recovery from sex addiction.

One client, riddled with shame, divulged that he had experienced a most disturbing and confusing message as a teen. His father, in need of blood transfusions, received tainted blood and died. The message from some of the members of his church was that his father had contracted AIDS and died due to some sin the teen committed. Can you imagine the sordid impact this message conveyed to this impressionable young man? His shame for sharing his sex addiction came with a dread of abandonment and rejection. Unfortunately, there was silence from the church that did not balance out that skewed message.

As a former church planter and pastor and one who experienced a painful church journey, I sat with mixed emotions. My heart broke for this young man's experience of severe pain and spiritual shunning. In addition, I was livid over how his church had handled him and felt re-injured concerning the way our church treated my wife and me in the past. Then, I felt even more compassion for him and relished being an instrument of grace, mercy, and compassion.

Although imperfect churches may be silent on the compassion, grace, and mercy of God, God himself is not, never will be, nor ever was silent. Francis Schaeffer has authored a book exhibiting this reality called *He Is There and He Is Not Silent* (1972). I have been on this journey with the Christian God for 44 years and my experience is very diverse. Not everyone practices a lifestyle of Christian transformation. Those who merely have a cursory awareness of God can skew or abuse truth in numerous ways. Those who are well seasoned at walking with God are not quick to make erroneous representations. Their natural tendency is to be compassionate and humble.

My associate and I have been working recently with a couple in conjoint therapy that experienced a silent distorted intimacy. I will call this couple Bill and Coleen. They had experienced another breach of trust due to his affair. Their mixed agenda for therapy consisted of her desire to see the relationship heal while his was to placate her so he could get the kind of "kinky, dirty, exciting sex" he wanted. This motive became evident in his individual session.

Her silent fear was of a final loss of the relationship, being abandoned, alone, and a failure as a spouse. His silent fear, evident in individual session, was that of not having truly meaningful intimacy. This was another case of sex becoming indistinguishable from intimacy. We discovered in a family-of-origin interview that he grew up in a chaotic, sexually free, hippie-like atmosphere, was unattended as a child, and learned to cope by consuming sex. In addition, he revealed that he had been hurt badly in a former relationship. He had come home early one evening to surprise his wife and found her in bed with his best friend. His already insecure attachment had been scarred by this destruction of his trust. But, his view of self as worthy hardened into "I'm going to get mine," and "to hell with others." He developed what one view of attachment theory calls an avoidant and dismissive style. As a child, he learned to ignore his internal state as unimportant or irrelevant to survival. As an adult he preferred to "keep the past in the past," as if somehow by ignoring it, it would not have a present influence. His controlling and avoiding kept him distant from his now traumatized spouse. He would bring her into his silent, distorted intimacy or end the relationship.

The Silence of Spiritual and Emotional Solitude

If it is true that approximately 30% of effective therapy is attributed to the quality of the therapeutic relationship (Thomas, 2006), then it behooves us first to attend to the mental, emotional, relational, and spiritual health of the practitioner. When I was a student at Richmont Graduate University, spiritual formation was a required area of general education. A significant outcome of that experience is my current daily practice of spiritual and emotional attunement. We learned numerous ways to help facilitate this by practicing the ancient church tradition of silence. Intentional solitude enables me to begin in a place of deeper knowing of my soul, being congruent first with self, with God, and with close others. These are intertwined and interdependent.

I have developed my personal practice of silence and solitude over 45 years of spiritual and emotional pilgrimage. I began some of these practices during my stint at Liberty University and Liberty Baptist Theological Seminary. These ancient spiritual church traditions have been created and used for the development of our internal life for over two millennia. The first is the Franciscan tradition with a primary focus on sensing God in the present. Knowledge of self, other, and God derives from present awareness of the senses. The second is the Augustinian tradition with a primary focus on intuition, allowing God to transform. This practice focuses on quiet contemplation and mindful being. The third is the Thomistic tradition with a primary focus on thinking as one explores and reflects upon the deeper personal meaning of the truth of God. A practice called *lectio divina* is a key ingredient to this means of spiritual formation. Fourth is the Ignatian tradition with a focus on the feeling of experiencing the love of God for us (Goehring, 2013). Practicing these disciplines as a lifestyle of desire motivated by love has enabled me to enter a place of internal calm, solace, and attunement that not only heightens my sense of internal awareness, but also puts me in a higher attunement with clients. My morning practices are critical to the effectiveness of my sessions regardless of when they occur.

In the morning, I get up in silence practicing deep breathing techniques, prepare myself for my walk of prayer and meditation, make coffee, turn on the You Version or Abide app on my phone, and spend the next 30 minutes or so attuning myself to the rhythms of my creator. Part of this entails listening quietly and reflectively to Hebrew wisdom literature—Psalms, Proverbs, Ecclesiastes, or the steamy, sensuous Song of Solomon. In these moments I experience the fears, doubts, longings, passions, anxieties, angers, losses, joys, and sorrows of ancient ones who experienced the wisdom, compassion, and presence of the Ultimate Attachment Figure. It is often reminiscent of being immersed in my clients' experiences. As I listen to these comforting words, they lift me up and align me properly with myself, God, and those close. I reflect, pray for myself and clients, and gain insights into working with clients. While contemplating, I find specific thoughts, emotions, or images come to mind. Often exercises that I create for group arise out of those times.

One instance occurred as I walked in listening silence. As I reflected on my men's group, an ancient Franciscan tradition came to mind that focuses on a sensory way of being with God. I developed a sensory awareness exercise that I implemented with my men's group. Part of the problem experienced was the tendency to compartmentalize self from self. Internal awareness is minimal due to addictions and attachment wounds. Since for much of their lives, clients experienced avoiding, numbing, or escaping, now that they do feel, it is difficult to know what to do with emotions. The new experience is positive, but often is unsettling and confusing and may trigger their addictive coping behaviors. This is one of our most powerful reasons for passionately insisting on full engagement in the group process. Group as a "good enough transitional attachment figure" provides them opportunity and freedom to identify, explore, and express a widening emotional experience in healthy ways.

The sensory awareness exercise I developed was implemented to further the integration of self with body, mind, and spirit. This exercise required a walk on the Greenway (a nature trail) near our office. The men were to walk 15 minutes out and 15 minutes back in silence. They were not to speak to one another or out loud. Instead, they were to seek to experience the walk with all of their senses: smell, sight, taste, touch, and hearing. They were to identify images, memories, reflections, thoughts, and feelings as they experienced the Greenway. We then spent group time processing those experiences. They were also asked to record what they had experienced in the form of images, thoughts, memories, and sensations while out on the trail.

During group processing they were asked to share what these images, memories, and sensations elicited. Each person acknowledged awkwardness with either the silence or the exercise and was more inclined to be on the Greenway because of the beautiful day. However, each man stated he had become more comfortable with silence and felt the benefit of a heightened sensory awareness. Many identified how this practice could help them attain a deeper level of internal calmness, emotional awareness, and a means of de-escalation.

The Silence of Pain, Loss, and Death

We have all experienced clients or personal events in which we have been touched, hindered, broken, devastated, or destroyed by a sliver, a wave, or an avalanche of pain, loss, or death in any form or a cocktail of assortments. Often it begins with a slow, silent, suffocating pain that comes from the dawning realization that something valuable has died.

Wilbur Ford had initially come because, he said, "My wife says I have a problem." After assessments and interviews, he was diagnosed with a porn addiction creating impairment in both self and his marriage. His silent shame kept him away from group until finally "trying" it. After he began, that silence melted in the context of the accepting "good enough attachment" atmosphere.

He began to establish sobriety and regain his wife Nancy's trust, while pressure grew in his occupation. His recovery plateaued. He continued in group but was not fully engaged. He relapsed after a year of sobriety. This disappointed him greatly, triggered his wife, and damaged trust. She felt vulnerable and betrayed again. He regained sobriety and established a greater level of honesty with group and conjoint therapy. Wilbur slipped again. This time not as drastically, but nonetheless, he went backwards. This time, he rebounded more quickly. However, Nancy became more skeptical, less trusting, and more suspicious. He continued to progress. She progressed in her own journey. Their couple's journey, however, was halted. They decided on a therapeutic separation.

Two months saw good progress. Then the fateful day occurred. Nancy found a stash of old porn DVDs that Wilbur had forgotten to destroy. Although he had not used them for over a year, that did not matter. It killed trust. This in no way impugns her or him. It is understandable that she felt betrayed. It is understandable that he felt exasperated. Wilbur sat in my office; the silent pain he had inflicted on his wife with each relapse, he now experienced in her silence. I was watching this man experience the death of himself and his relationship with his wife, as he sat in silence at the turn of events. I was silent. For what could I say to console him? What could I say to encourage him with her journey? What could I do but sit in silence with him? The sad truth is that it was not just he, but she as well who felt the deafening silence of the pain of attachment wounds, betrayal, disconnection, and loss of emotional safety and bonding. This client has been with me for almost three years now and as such is close to my heart. Part of me wants to wave a magic therapy wand to bring about the healing. The other part of me realizes that it may ultimately be through more pain that full healing comes. David Benner writes,

> Taking up our cross requires that we accept the realities of our life that we wish were otherwise. As Richard Rohr reminds us: "God is found in the actual—not in the idealized." There is no need to change the circumstances of our life, even of our heart, in order to meet God. But we must first accept reality. God is far too real to be found anywhere else (Benner, 2015, p. 92).

Whether the silence is unwanted, unwelcomed, desired, treasured, avoided or embraced, it is a reality of the human condition, a teacher of the soul, if we allow ourselves to embrace it with a curious mind and willing heart. When I was first presented with the opportunity to write this article, I literally paused in silence and thought, "That is an odd subject for therapy but maybe has merit." Since then, I have reflected and become more emotionally and mentally attuned to silence. I have come to a new and greater appreciation of how cathartic it can be and how loud it often speaks in sessions. My heart's cry now is, "Let me be even more attuned to the message it conveys and respond in the most therapeutic way possible in that moment with that client."

References

Benner, D. G. (2015). *Desiring God's will* (Expanded edition ed.). Downers Grove, IL: InterVarsity Press.

Goehring, M. (2013). Traditions of Christian spiritual formation. In *Richmont Graduate School of Counseling traditions of Christian spiritual formation* (pp. 15-40). Atlanta, GA: Richmont Graduate University.

Schaeffer, F. A. (1972). *He is there and he is not silent.* Wheaton, IL: Tyndale House.

Thomas, M. L. (2006, March 24). The contributing factors of change in a therapeutic process. *Contemporary Family Therapy, 28*, 201-210. https://doi.org/DOI 10.1007/s10591-006-9000-4

Commentary

THE AUTHOR TOUCHES ON A NUMBER OF RELATIONSHIP ASPECTS THAT ARE NECESSARY for a safe and self-reflective process in therapy. However, my reaction to his discussion of spirituality is feeling the invasion of religion into otherwise good practice. I was raised Southern Baptist and attended church twice every Sunday and usually on Wednesday evenings. I found that there was no value placed on self-reflection. "God" was a cudgel to force compliance and a way of escaping threats, especially of dying. Self-punishment was encouraged rather than understanding. Hypocrisy was frequently on display and there was no room for questioning dogma. As a result, I am very skeptical of spirituality being presented as a necessary component of recovery or stopping unwanted behavior.

The generic form of spirituality that 12-Step programs offer appears to be helpful to some, but others are turned off and have to ignore it in order to stay in the group.

I appreciate the author's revelations about his experience with religion and not endorsing inhumanity inflicted in the name of God. I support the methods described for centering and self-reflecting by the therapist, especially before and after a group session. I disagree that it must be couched in spiritual or religious terms, and in fact believe that it will be a detriment to treatment for some clients.

It is a very delicate matter to work with someone's spiritual beliefs without imposing our own biases, and thus I allow the client to lead any discussion of religion or spirituality. Silence can be experienced by clients as an opening, or as unspoken assent or judgment. I value my ability to tolerate silence as a crucial skill that creates space for client self-reflection. I also find that silence allows associations to bubble up that might be useful to the client or to me.

I see what the author calls "sex addiction" as an attachment problem expressed in the pursuit of superficial and instrumental connections with others. The "addict" does not know that there is the possibility of a deeper connection in which co-regulation and security can occur. "Team" is a superficial concept, and secrecy is the norm. Sex can be preoccupying, especially if it is dangerous, but then the void of disconnection returns and the search begins for a new, possibly even more dangerous experience. The addict has learned that going to another for support and connection is empty and possibly emotionally or physically dangerous. Some learn to ignore inner yearnings to the point that they are walled off from consciousness, while others feel the pain of attachment anxiety and pursue connection self-destructively. This leads to focusing on what the other can provide, not on what one can provide for oneself, and to pseudo-empathy. There is no self-reflection because there was little or no interest in his or her interior growing up.

One of the first barriers to treatment is the perception that one will have the same experience of the unavailability of the therapist. Thus, having a significant other learn about secret behavior may be the main reason for starting, but needs to be replaced by self-reflection with the therapist and eventually the group. Eventually, the addict can share with their partner, who hopefully has differentiated in their own work. If the partner has not done their own work, they may unconsciously encourage relapse, possibly through judgment and overreaction, which remind the addict to not disclose their inner world. The presence of significant secrets is a hallmark of relapse. The couple dynamic is crucial to long term recovery.

—Lee Blackwell, PhD

Reply

I CAN APPRECIATE BLACKWELL'S SENSE THAT THE FOCUS ON SPIRITUALITY FELT LIKE AN INVASION OF RELIGION, since, in the article, I do not allude to the fact that in all my advertisement, listings in various memberships, and information on our website, I clearly articulate that I work from a Judeo-Christian worldview. I do also communicate to every client my full frame of reference in doing therapy—family systems, attachment-focused, EFT-oriented, former pastor, and long term recovering sex addict (when appropriate). I also convey that I have the ability to proceed in any of those directions based upon the client's autonomous decisions. In my group settings, we advertise clearly two types of sex addiction recovery groups. One is faith-friendly, having those who have no interest in religion, but see value in spirituality, a Jewish orientation, a higher power orientation, or Christianity. The other sex addiction recovery group that we do is specifically Christian in its orientation. With regards to the sources of spirituality notions, techniques, and practices, focus has been placed on this audience of fellow psychotherapists in order to provide references for accessing some of these excellent resources that may enhance one's practice.

I would argue that fewer and fewer therapists function from the notion that we can practice from a neutral position, with no bias. Theoretically, that was advocated earlier in the history of psychotherapy, but has been more recently acknowledged that it is an untenable position. It is also a position taught less and less as a standard in graduate therapy programs. We all have biases and often convey them in unconscious ways. I do, however, assert with Blackwell that we should not impose our biases on clients. This, as an integrated lifestyle practice—as is spirituality—is communicated to every client through tone, eye contact, body language, emotional/spiritual attunement, appropriate touch, empathetic listening, and when needed, words.

I concur with Blackwell on being familiar with experiences, indirectly and directly, that exhibited unattractive and even harmful attributes of those who were supposed to represent a more gracious persona after the founder of their faith. I have also witnessed the harmful effects of those who implement an impersonal set of laws versus exhibiting a dynamic relationship with the founder. The important thing to know is that there are many places that practice the latter and are growing in their awareness of helping those who I see in my area of sex addiction recovery specialization.

I must admit that I am a little foggy on the full significance of Blackwell's comments concerning the "addict." What I have observed in clinical experience is that the addict's impaired ways of attaching, which they are generally not even aware of initially, are unconscious cries for meaningful connection. As John Bowlby identified so clearly in his attachment theory, we are hardwired for connection. As I have worked with clients individually, in group, and in couple's recovery work, it has been very rewarding to begin to see this buried self begin to awaken and learn self-regulation from exposure to the therapist and in group. For those who have experienced a certain level of secure attachment early in their lives, the process can unfold much sooner. For those who were imprinted in a chaotic or abusive environment, the process is very slow and filled with setbacks. For some it is extremely difficult and slow. They experience a growing sense that self is worthy/lovable and that safe others are trustworthy. When this begins to happen on a regular basis, they begin to reclaim, or claim for the first time, a healthy view of self and others, and experience healing.

—Bruce Wayne Knight, LMFT, LPCA, CSAT, CST, MDiv, MAMFT,

▼

Befriending Silence in Therapy

Steven Abell

Gina's Wisdom

WHILE I LOVE THE ACADEMIC STUDY OF PSYCHOLOGY AND TEACH AT A MID-SIZE UNIVERSITY, CLINICAL PRACTICE HAS TAUGHT ME THE MOST ABOUT THE PSYCHOLOGY OF YOUNG CHILDREN AND THEIR CAREGIVERS. My clinical practice also keeps me humble. Every time I think I have a solid understanding of psychotherapeutic theory or child development, I encounter a young client who causes me to realize the limitations of my knowledge. I tell my students that clinical practice, when it involves hours of listening and careful observation with young children, is what teaches us the most about child psychology.

If I am honest, however, I must also admit that certain aspects of clinical practice have been difficult for me. I like to be in dialogue with others and generally prefer company to solitude. My professional and family lives are busy, and I often have a to-do list that feels ominously long. I wonder if my incessant busyness is really a way to avoid the discomfort of solitude and the silence I need to ponder and process clinical interactions. It is hard to consider my clients' lives in an optimal way when I hear a cacophony of competing voices. In recent years, I worry that my inability to regulate the technology in my life (cell phones, the Internet, etc.) has made this situation worse. I know I have often failed to appreciate the value of silence in my life and work as a psychotherapist. As I reflect on this, I am struck in particular by my work with a young girl named Gina, who at times mystified and frustrated me but ultimately taught me a lesson about the value and purpose of silence.

When the father of this child (whom I will call Mr. Y) first called me, I was struck immediately by the high level

STEVEN ABELL, PhD, has been a professor of psychology at the University of Detroit Mercy for more than 20 years. His favorite things about the university are the diversity of the student body and the presence of some very supportive colleagues in his department. He also has a psychotherapy practice focusing on children and their families. His loving wife is also a clinical psychologist, and they have been blessed with three children.
abellsc@udmercy.edu

of anxiety in his voice. I am accustomed to speaking with extremely worried, anxious parents, but there was a particularly distressed and even desperate quality in the voice of Mr. Y. He shared with me that his wife had died several months previously after a difficult illness. His daughter Gina was currently 8 years old, and Mr. Y was worried about the emotional impact of the mother's death on his daughter. The father also shared with me that Gina was an only child who had been born to her parents somewhat late in life. Mr. Y's tremendous love and concern for his daughter were apparent even over the phone. He also expressed considerable guilt and remorse that he had not arranged mental health services for his daughter sooner. Mr. Y had "at last," in his words, called the family's pediatrician, who gave him my number. I told Mr. Y that I thought any delay was more than understandable given the overwhelming nature of coping with his wife's illness and death. He seemed to appreciate this comment, and we arranged an initial appointment to discuss his daughter.

Mr. Y presented in person as a very polished, professionally dressed man in his early 50s. He described in painful detail, however, the nature of his wife's illness and his tremendous anxiety about whether he would be able to meet his daughter's needs as a single parent. Prior to his wife's illness, Mr. Y indicated that they had maintained relatively traditional gender roles in their marriage, and he now felt ill-prepared to be a primary parent. To cope with this situation, Mr. Y had taken dramatic steps to reduce the number of hours he worked in a demanding career, and he also described significant support from extended family. Mr. Y also shared that he had lost a parent himself as a child, and that this loss had been extremely traumatic for him. He was heartbroken by the thought that his beloved only child might share this experience. While I understood Mr. Y's concern for his daughter, I was also concerned about his own process of grief and tremendously high anxiety. I found myself feeling a bit relieved at the end of the interview when Mr. Y readily accepted a referral for his own individual treatment with a trusted colleague. We also made an appointment for me to have an initial meeting a few days later with his daughter. Our plan was for me to begin working individually with Gina and to have periodic child-guidance sessions with Mr. Y.

When Gina initially came to my office with her father, I found her a pleasant and well-mannered young girl, beautifully dressed in a fashionable play outfit with long hair neatly combed and braided. The father had expressed to me that Gina, despite her mother's illness and death, continued to do very well in the elite elementary school she attended. I was not surprised by this, given her calm demeanor and seeming comfort around adults. She easily separated from her father to come back to my office and politely answered some of my routine questions about her school, her neighborhood, etc. Gina and I discussed briefly my knowledge of her family background, and she even volunteered a few details about her mother's illness and death. I showed her the toys and art supplies for children in my office, but she expressed a desire to play cards for the rest of the session as we spoke about her situation.

Gina's initial presentation, however, did nothing to prepare me for the challenges of our work together, as I began to find it extremely difficult to form an alliance with her, or to feel that positive things were being accomplished in our work. Early in my career I had worked full-time for several years with children and adolescents in a residential treatment center. This work accustomed me to children with a history of severe trauma, so I am generally not surprised when it takes time to form a therapeutic alliance (though many of the children in my outpatient practice are healthier and form a ther-apeutic alliance more easily than the children I worked with in residential care). I am also accustomed to children, or especially adolescents, who are very angry and defiantly remain silent for a considerable period of time. But I was unprepared for Gina to come in week after week, and then month after month, and say almost nothing. I was puzzled and perplexed by Gina's silence, and even more confused that her facial expression and body language conveyed none of the angry silence of a defiant child, or even the des-perate efforts at personal control that lead some children from chaotic families to stop talking. Gina would come in every week, hand me the deck of playing cards from a toy bin in the office, and announce the game she wanted to play that day (she knew lots of children's card games). I tried initially to ask her different questions, but her answers be-came increasingly brief and dismissive. Not only did Gina say little, but she also seemed to have no interest in expressive play or art work. The carefully selected toys, dolls, and art supplies in my office went unused. As time went on, Gina and I would spend almost entire sessions silently playing card games like eights and gin rummy, exchanging little more than perfunctory greetings when she came and pleasant good-byes when she left. At times I felt helpless and ineffectual in the face of her silence, and worried that her family's time and money were not being put to good use.

My confusion about the case increased when I met with Gina's father for child-guid-ance sessions. Though his anxiety began to decrease slightly over time, Mr. Y continued to be a highly anxious and worried parent. Before I could say much, Mr. Y would volun-teer that he was so pleased that I was seeing his daughter, and that Gina mentioned to him frequently how much she enjoyed coming. By the father's report, Gina was always in a content and happy mood as they drove to my office. I would have understood this reported enthusiasm a bit better had Gina been even slightly more interactive in her sessions. In my practice, I most often see enthusiasm for therapy when I work with emo-tionally neglected children who are desperate for the undivided attention of an empath-ic adult. Gina, however, was doted on by her father as well as concerned extended family in the area. It was hard for me to reconcile how completely shut down Gina seemed during our sessions with the father's description of her positive feelings about treatment. Despite many years of working with parents, I could not for the life of me figure out a diplomatic and empathic way to broach this subject with Mr. Y, as I worried greatly about doing anything that might increase his sense of anxiety.

One additional bit of confusion I experienced had to do with the passage of time during Gina's sessions. Despite the silence, I found strangely that I was not bored, nor did time seem to pass slowly. When I am with court-ordered, adult clients who lack intrinsic motivation, I have occasionally felt bored or that time dragged. Sometimes I think a psychotherapist's experience of ennui may be in response to a lack of true mo-tivation on the client's part. Despite the apparent lack of activity in my sessions with Gina, I had a strange feeling at times that she was somehow engaged in the process. On other occasions, however, I believed this sense of possible purpose was just wishful thinking on my part.

After well over a year of weekly sessions with Gina, I had resigned myself to the fact that our silent psychotherapy sessions might go on for a very long time. Then Gina did something totally unexpected. She came into my office on a cold day and, while remov-ing her winter coat, took a small framed picture out of her pocket. Without saying a

Gina's Wisdom　　　**57**

word, she carefully placed the picture on an end table. The photograph was a rather formal, professional portrait of a pleasant looking, middle-aged woman. Gina then sat on a sofa by the table. After a few moments of stunned and awkward silence, I managed rather haltingly to say:

"Oh, is that a picture of your mother?"

"Yes."

"Did you bring it from home?"

"Yes, I keep it in a drawer in my dresser."

"Oh, I see, and you decided to bring it to our session today?"

"Well, yes." (Gina was always polite, but from the look on her face, she clearly thought the answer to my last question was pretty obvious).

Then, feeling I could perhaps take a small chance, I said, "Would you like to speak about your mother a bit today?"

No response. Gina got up without saying a word, walked over to the toy bin and found the usual deck of playing cards. As she handed me the cards, she said, "Let's play gin rummy," and that was her last utterance until she put the cards away at the end of the hour, carefully zipped her mother's picture back in the pocket of her winter coat, and politely said good-bye as usual.

For many months, this silent ritual continued. Gina always placed her mother's picture in a loving and careful way on the end table, and gingerly zipped it back in a coat pocket before she left. During child-guidance sessions, the father reported that Gina had become more assertive at home in terms of stating her wishes about her mother's memory. Gina rather firmly expressed that she wanted her father and extended relatives to stop asking her so frequently how she was doing or how well she was coping with the loss of her mother. She began to decline to go with her father on his frequent visits to the mother's gravesite but indicated that she did wish to decorate the mother's grave before Christmas and on the anniversary of the mother's birthday. She also wanted to continue decorating her home extensively for major holidays, something that had reportedly been very important to her mother.

Mr. Y's description of her newly assertive behavior at home gave me an opportunity to reassure him that Gina, despite the profound loss she had suffered, would be ok. Mr. Y began to see that the constant questions about her welfare and how she was coping were not helpful, and that he and others needed to focus more on the details of her daily life. Over a long period of time, Mr. Y was also able to use his own therapy to process and contain some anxiety and grief, which allowed him to be more relaxed around Gina. After seven or eighths months of bringing her mother's picture to every therapy session, Gina abruptly stopped this behavior, again with little explanation or comment on her part.

Finally, after a long time, I began to realize that while I had been confused by some of Gina's behavior in treatment, she was actually a very precocious child. In fact, I am convinced that she was wise before her time. I think Gina was wise in the sense that she knew a great deal about her own emotional needs. I had worried for months that I was unable to help Gina come to terms psychologically with her mother's death. Perhaps I had also allowed myself to be too influenced by the father's anxiety. I believe now that Gina was processing her mother's death to the very best of her ability. What she needed was for the adults around her to respect her autonomy and burgeoning emotional capabilities. Gina needed accompaniment more than interpretation or catharsis. Despite the mother's tragic illness and death, I came to suspect that Gina's mother must have managed to give her daughter an exceptional amount of love and care during the time they had together, so that in some ways Gina was unusually confident and self-assured for a child of her age.

Before working with Gina, I thought I knew a lot about the possible meanings of silence in children and adolescents, but she reminded me that I still have a great deal to learn. I believe the child psychoanalyst D.W. Winnicott might have had some powerful insights into the nature of Gina's silence. Winnicott (1958) discussed how we learn to be alone by being left in a quiescent state in the presence of a non-intrusive other. Perhaps Gina was learning how to grieve, and she had a powerful sense of how to accomplish this. She simply did not want to have to be engaged in this process all by herself. What Gina liked about her sessions was that she was able to get me to be silent, so that she could process her grief in the presence of another, but on her terms and without too much intrusion. When treatment ended after several years, I was convinced that in her silence, Gina was actually finding her voice. I will not be surprised if she someday becomes an eloquent writer or highly articulate public speaker. In her wisdom, Gina knew she needed time and space to own her emotional experience, and that silence was an essential part of this journey. ▼

Reference

Winnicott, D.W. (1958). The capacity to be alone. *The International Journal of Psychoanalysis, 39*, 416-420.

In human intercourse the tragedy begins, not when there is misunderstanding about words, but when silence is not understood.
—Henry David Thoreau

Silence:
Healing the Hidden Darkness in Psychotherapy

Omar "Nick" B

The concept of silence in therapy carries two meanings, each distinct and opposing. These meanings, which I argue comprise the healing journey of the therapist from darkness to light, will be the focal point of this article, informed primarily by the work of the late psychologist Kenneth Wapnick, my teacher and mentor. I offer personal reflections from my own journal writings as the backdrop for the themes presented, which will be further elaborated upon through an examination of the work of Ernest Becker. Excerpts from the letters of Rainer Maria Rilke and the poetry of William Blake, along with Wapnick, will round out the portrait of silence here presented.

OMAR "NICK" BUSTOS, PHD, LMFT, is a California licensed marriage and family therapist with a doctorate in clinical psychology. He works in a school district special-education setting providing psychotherapy for students and families impacted by serious mental health challenges. He maintains a private practice in Temecula, California, and is an adjunct professor at California Institute for Human Science in Encinitas. He is a devoted husband, father and lover of classical music.
nicomar222@gmail.com

Prologue: The Psychotherapy Ideal

THE RECOGNITION OF OUR ONENESS WITH CLIENTS IS THE ULTIMATE EXPRESSION OF HEALING IN PSYCHOTHERAPY. It implies our withdrawal from the ego's foundation of disunity and separation to allow the inner experience of unitive love, in which therapist and client are joined as one. In relevant discourse this experience takes on a decidedly spiritual tone, manifested lucidly in the work of Kenneth Wapnick (2017), preeminent scholar of the psychologically-informed spiritual path of *A Course in Miracles*. As Wapnick (2006) writes, poetically describing the spiritual ideal of psychotherapy: "What, in the end, is psychotherapy but the sweet harmony in which therapist and patient begin as two individuals, and ultimately blend their voices into the sounds of love's healing music—the melody of gentle silence?" (p. 421).

Whereas therapists are typically occupied with the external *form* of therapy practice, Wapnick always points back to its inner healing aspect, or *content*. The content, explains Wapnick (1980), denotes the transegoic region beyond the spatial and temporal constraints of the ego's disharmonious world where love's gentle silence shines ever brightly, transforming the therapy office into a "temple... [where] all dreams of separation and inequality are dispelled" (p. 50). The recognition that our clients are not separate but, rather, joined with us, is an experience in equal measure transformative and humbling, marked by the awareness that healing, despite our ego's grandiose aims to the contrary, may come *through us* but never does it originate *from us*. Yet this awareness requires a confrontation with the limits of our identification with the ego, a conflict which takes us to the very root of who we think we are. Though we may believe our therapeutic identity to be rooted in nobility and selflessness, the truth may not be so simple. For healing within this context requires an undoing of the parts of ourselves known precisely to be the mechanisms that we instinctively draw upon in serving others. Thus, getting our ego out of the way—which I believe to be the prime imperative within any therapeutic endeavor—implies a process of growth, within which silence, as the manifestation of both the light and darkness within us, plays a vital role.

The Fear of Joining: A Reflection

I begin with an excerpt from my own journal writings, where I describe the anxiety of being with another:

At times, in session, the familiar guard shows up, shielding me against the open nakedness of the moment—those aspects of myself that lay rotten and wasted, and hide among darkness and shadows. I anxiously take stock, and find the uncertainty of the present too much to bear. And so, I infuse the space between myself and the client with raucous mental movement, usually taking the form of labored, heady analysis, righteous certainty or reliance on past associations. When I am silent to my authentic voice, the one panged by vulnerability, insecurity, fear and confusion—yet within this, the gateway to meeting the heart of another in loving fullness—the psychotherapy encounter becomes another grim testament to the law of separation that governs the ego's world.

A primary theme here is the inability to tolerate the discomfort, the "open nakedness" of the moment, in which I place a wall between myself and the client, made of "raucous mental movement." Denying my pain and vulnerability drives the conflict, resulting in psychotherapy performed in a spirit of self-denial and clinical arrogance rather than openness and humility, the precursors to genuine healing. It is this conflicted inner dynamic which will now be more closely examined.

The Ego's Silence: The Vital Lie

If the "melody of gentle silence" (2006, p. 421) in psychotherapy, as Wapnick discusses, hearkens to its ultimate healing expression, there yet exists, as illustrated above, a contrasting silence which bespeaks not joining, but instead separation and disharmony. What may account for this darkened silence? A look into the hidden aspects of our humanity, those typically denied while acting within our professional roles, lends relevant clues.

Ernest Becker, in his seminal work *The Denial of Death* (1973) and posthumous follow-up *Escape From Evil* (1975), penetratingly articulates the ugly truth that lies at the core of the human psyche: that of the ever-present, but generally unconscious, awareness of death, which stalks the mind in awful perpetuity, forcing individuals to create elaborate, society-affirming costumes designed to defend against the terror of a painfully limited existence. Put starkly, reality, argues Becker, "is simply refusing to acknowledge that... death [is] constantly with us" (1973, p. 17). Thus, the mind seeks to flee its desperate fate, erecting a falsified image of the self built to forestall the awareness of its own vulnerability. Becker continues, introducing the idea of the "vital lie":

> This despair he avoids by building defenses; and these defenses allow him to feel a basic sense of self-worth, of meaningfulness, of power... We called one's life style a *vital lie*, and now we can understand better why we said it was vital: it is a *necessary* and basic dishonesty about oneself and one's whole situation... (p. 55).

The urge to establish some semblance of psychological continuity amid an ultimately bleak existence is universal; it is the lynchpin holding together the ego-self as we know it. As long as identification with the ego-self persists, one is shackled within the prison of this internalized dynamic.

Individuals may reinforce the vital lie through the attainment of professional credibility, building a repertoire of relative success and prestige whose fundamental purpose is reinforcing the myth of perpetual selfhood. Professional psychotherapy, as such, may aptly be used in the service of the vital lie, an effective and aggrandizing counterweight against the emptiness at the core of the self. We would be naïve in thinking that our minds, as therapists, are somehow untouched by the trappings of the ego's terror of annihilation. Another excerpt from my personal journal makes the point:

> *Psychotherapy may, at times, serve as a way for me to defend against my humanity rather than embrace it, and I thusly transform the pain of others into a ritual of self-congratulatory effort, a trophy to myself and my own fragile illusions.*

Though we may (of necessity, to be sure) present a face of competence and expertise, this merely hides the reality of our limitations. In fact, the urge to "heal others" may have its origin within a particularly malicious, albeit unconscious, mindset. In *Escape From Evil*, Becker forwards insight initially presented in *The Denial of Death* but goes further, offering the premise that preservation of the self is won through ego-inflating social rituals endorsed and upheld by the dominant culture, and, most effectively carried out against other people. Our own unique image of power and prestige *must be* won at the expense of another—as Becker writes, "you cannot force your status vis-à-vis someone else *unless there is a someone else*" (italics added, p. 13). Our urge to help and heal may, therefore, point to a deeper need for self-renewal, through which we use clients to serve our own interests. Again, to merely *live and exist* as a seemingly separate self, according to Becker, is to promulgate this conflicted interpersonal dynamic.

Thus, I offer a foundational belief within the therapeutic mindset which bears examination: that of the therapist's own vulnerability, which of necessity leads to the terrifying belief in his inability to effect change in any real way. I argue it is this shameful terror which comprises the therapist's *unconscious* existence and is an inescapable fact of his professional persona. No training, no certification, no experience can effectively cover the utter frailty that lies at the center of the therapist's very identity. We may defend against this by embarking on training after training, certification after certification, hoping against hope to somehow appease the gnawing sense that deep down, *I don't know what I'm doing and I truly don't know how to help anyone.*

Naturally, this creates a tormented view of both the client and therapeutic process. By this I mean that we must perceive our client as an adversary: the one who so desperately needs our help, but for whom we are at a loss to offer anything truly of value—a further reminder of our own mortal woundedness. And so, resentment for our client *must* result, though likely repressed when things appear to be going well, but eventually rearing forth when treatment stalls. A journal entry further describing my own conflicts

Silence: Healing the Hidden Darkness in Psychotherapy

illustrates this dynamic:

> To expand upon a primary factor in my discomfort in working with others—the annoyance, resistance and anxiety that emerges—one thing that comes up are feelings of resentment toward the person that needs help. In acknowledging that I cannot help them and the inevitable lethargy and hopelessness that results, a temptation is to fault them for having the problem... This leads to silent accusations (against them) of weakness and condemnation. My inadequacy breeds hatred of others. For if they come to me for help and I cannot, then they must be the problem and will become the object of my scorn.

I continue, now expressing in more detail the mechanism behind this painful inner movement—the silent denial of my own vulnerability:

> Thus, when I am silent to the reality of my own limitations, when it seems that the "I" of me, locked behind a mask of professionalism and clinical distance, is the face which I offer my clients, then the session becomes a graveyard, hearkening to a listless spiritual emptiness. My interventions are rote and uninspired, borne of a bitter and cold intellectualization, and my client is reduced to the sum of his or her parts. And the space between us, whose true essence is a diffuse boundary, becomes instead a great wall, a divide which bespeaks separation and hierarchy—therapist above, client below. Silence, in this sense, is equated with loneliness and dread, for in these moments I am locked in a cocoon made of my judgments, my very limited point of view, the reflections of which bounce back toward me within an intrapsychic hall of mirrors. And I am burdened by the weight of it all. For to be responsible for my client under these terribly inadequate conditions is to be overcome by a penetrating helplessness. How could I, or anyone for that matter, offer anything remotely resembling healing when the dirge of separation reigns?

From this limited vantage point our only solution is to remain aloof and silent to the pain and vulnerability of our own experience—after all, we must be steadfast within our role in accordance with professional standards, no matter our internal state. Yet, to be silent to the vulnerability that is exposed as we work with people is to be in denial about our actual condition: that of the messy and frightening reality we share with our clients, not necessarily in form, but certainly in content. And how could we ever hope to assist people in authentically reflecting upon their own lives when we, the helpers, are silent to our own terrible moorings?

Yet the ego-self, the aspect of our mind which is tethered to the thought of separation, in its grandiosity never allows the exposure of its precarious condition—that is, of its inherent nothingness. Like a person drowning and wildly fighting for breath, the ego's prime motivation is its own survival. This is a dynamic that is commonly underscored in spiritual or contemplative literature (Roberts, 1991, 2005; Wapnick, 2017), and which is clearly manifest in our interactions with clients. While we are silent to the guilt and pain in ourselves, we are inescapably doomed to the repression and projection of these unconscious forces. And we see our clients not for who they are, but as shadows of our own guilt, and our interventions follow from there. We thus cut ourselves off from the ability to truly join with our clients by refusing to acknowledge our own fear and helplessness, precisely the emotional contours that we share with them.

Is there a way to escape the clutches of our silence, the withdrawal from the awareness that the vulnerability of the client is, in content, our own?

The Silence of Healing

We have up 'til now examined the influence of the ego's darkened silence—the denial of our vulnerability and limitations—upon the psychotherapy process. And while the dangers inherent in acting primarily from an ego standpoint are evident, there is yet another way available to us. How is this reached? A passage from the letters of poet Rainer Maria Rilke (trans. 2009) provides a starting point:

> The person who has not, in a moment of firm resolve, accepted—yes, even rejoiced in—what has struck him with terror—he has never taken possession of the full, ineffable power of our existence (p. 87).

Rilke here articulates a helpful theme in developing a broadened mindset within the therapeutic interaction: the ability to face up to the "terror" of existence, which as we have seen is deeply embedded within the treatment dyad as it is in life itself. To "rejoice" in what has "struck [us] with terror" (p. 87), poetically articulates a sense of quiet acceptance, allowing terror to be as it is, in openness and humility. Becker, in *The Denial of Death*, provides similar thinking on the matter, suggesting that our natural existential grief offers us an opportunity for growth and learning:

> The flood of anxiety is not the end for man. It is, rather, a 'school' that provides man with the ultimate education, the final maturity... Once you face up to it, it reveals the truth of your situation; and only by seeing that truth can you pen a new possibility for yourself" (p. 87-89).

The suggestion, therefore, is to generate a willingness within ourselves to look at the whole of our lives, specifically those places of darkness and desolation which, to our detriment, we have conditioned ourselves to turn against. Thus, to look is to probe the deeper regions of the mind, no longer denying our limitations but instead embracing what they can teach us. Here again, in another letter, Rilke offers wise insights, now discussing a more accepting attitude where all things, even the fearful thought of death and annihilation, are included as a manifestation within the grand movement of life.

> I am not saying that we should love death, but rather that we should love life so generously, without picking and choosing, that we automatically include it (life's other half) in our love. This is what actually happens in the great expansiveness of love, which cannot be stopped or constricted. It is only because we exclude it that death becomes more and more foreign to us and, ultimately, our enemy (p. 86).

Thus, it is love, described by Rilke as expansive and momentous, that wishes to include all things in its embrace and makes no distinctions among the objects of its perception. It is this love that bridges the gap between us and the terror of annihilation. And so, the question: How may this be applied in our relationship with clients?

We return to Kenneth Wapnick (2006), now offering a parallel discussion dedicated to the psychotherapy dynamic, who tells us that love is ever present in the mind of the therapist if only he or she can *be still*:

> It is when therapists are able to remind themselves that love waits quietly beyond the clouds of guilt, fear, and attack, and all they need do is be that presence of quiet patience, that healing occurs. They indeed do nothing but be still (p. 419).

He equates *stillness* with *silence*, "the soundless song of love" in which the selfish identities we previously cherished now "fade and disappear" (p. 419). Thus, it is the transmutation of the shameful silence of the ego into a genuine silence, "the sounds of love's healing music" (p. 421), that allows this embracing love-sense to come forth and heal the divisions between ourselves and our clients. Silence, now imbued with an altogether different meaning from which we learn to become quiet to the voice of the ego within, helps us forge a new path. Wapnick offers more insight:

> What had heretofore been conceived in guilt and fear becomes transformed into harmonies of love and healing; the cacophonous world of hate having given way to the sweet sounds of music; the melody of love we sing first to each other metamorphoses as the eternal song we have always sung as spirit (p. 420).

And so we learn, little by little, to turn toward our vulnerability and not away from it, and let love's gentle silence remind us that the client's pain and fear is our own. In another brief entry, I write:

> *I forget, and must be reminded, that the healing movement depends on my willingness to confront my own darkness and surrender it to the sweet, still space where mind is joined with mind, and heart with heart.*

We need not fix or change the hurt or sadness, but instead let love's silent song remind us that we are joined, in spirit, with our clients. And from this space our interventions now carry a healing fragrance and a whisper of peace. We are not needy for our clients to change, for we have withdrawn our investment in the outcome. We no longer use our clients as a means toward the resolution of our own conflicts, as now we see that we are no different, in content, from them. In our joining are the conditions for healing met, for now our minds are made free from the imprisoning influence of the ego and its anxiety-denying machinations. And now are we free to *let healing be* (*A Course in Miracles*, 1992, p. 172). As the savior-figure in William Blake's poem "On Another's Sorrow" (1974) demonstrates, to love is to sit with the pain of another, with total commitment and in total devotion. Here are salient excerpts from the poem:

...Think not thou canst sigh a sigh
And thy Maker is not by;
Think not thou canst weep a tear
And thy Maker is not near.

O! he gives to us his joy
That our grief he may destroy;
Till our grief is fled and gone
He doth sit by us and moan. (p. 98)

The last two lines of the final stanza offer a moving portrayal of the oneness of love. The loving figure has no needs, no agenda, no other purpose than to give of himself, totally. It is this all-inclusive love, therefore, that I believe can infuse even the most ordinary of circumstances in therapy if we can just, as Wapnick says, *be still*. Yet the process involves gently confronting our own needs and anxieties—the sorrowful silence of the ego—which, as we have seen, we reflexively project upon our clients. In the silence of love our minds are open to healing and wholeness, and it is this, in content, that we now share with others.

Concluding Thoughts

It is important to recognize that the healing potential of any psychotherapy encounter will be diminished unless the central issue of the therapist's ego, with its propensity for self-aggrandizement and self-delusion, is seen and let go. This, more than any other dynamic, determines the flow of the therapy process, and consequently, its outcome. We, as therapists, must never forget that healing does not come from us but rather, flows through us, and manifests in direct correspondence with our willingness to get out of the way. While we may be trained in any number of modalities and have accrued years or decades of experience, the fact remains: it is the love in us, which transcends temporal and spatial boundaries, that heals, and allows us to perceive the oneness which, in truth, we share with our clients.

We, therefore, must readily and courageously accept whatever ego-based needs we bring to our professional roles—the need to be the authority, the need to be right, the need to be liked and loved, the need to be helpful—and realize that these blocks will inevitably forestall our ability to be truly helpful. For we will use our clients, albeit unconsciously, to satisfy our needs, and subtly tailor our interactions with them in the service of the protection of our self-concept. Simply stated, psychotherapy practiced in the service of the ego becomes all too human, dripping with the scent of a dark frailty that bespeaks an unfortunate shadowy cycle of repression and projection.

In my own experience, this painful dynamic is resolved when I am reminded that I am not the healer; rather, it is the true healer—the silence of love within—to which I must surrender, wherein the memory of love breaks through and embraces the client and myself as one. I conclude with a final offering from my own writings, with words inspired by my teacher, Kenneth Wapnick:

It is the content that heals, that informs a truly therapeutic movement between therapist and client. And this feeling is one that is informed, in its truest essence, by Silence, that creative space, brimming with potentiality, attested to by the unmistakeable feeling of joining with another. In that Silence my pain and the pain of my client dissolves, and all that is felt is the loving oneness between us. My interventions become the obvious outgrowth of this fullness of Love, but it is not the words that heal. It is the content, which carries the song of mercy and forgiveness, that is communicated, and my client, previously a separate fragment in a tomb made of flesh, now becomes my brother with whom I join at the altar of Love. ▼

References

A Course in Miracles: Combined volume. (2nd ed.). (1992). Mill Valley, CA: Foundation for Inner Peace.

Becker, E. (1973). *The denial of death.* New York: The Free Press.

Becker, E. (1975). *Escape from evil.* New York: The Free Press.

Blake, W. (1974). *The portable Blake.* (A. Kazin, Ed.) New York: Penguin Books.

Rilke, R. M. *A year with Rilke: Daily readings from the best of Rainer Maria Rilke.* (A. Barrows, & J. Macy, Trans.) Toronto, ON, Canada: HarperCollins Publishers Ltd.

Roberts, B. (1991). *The path to no-self: Life at the center.* Albany, NY: SUNY Press.

Roberts, B. (2005). *What is self? A study of the spiritual journey in terms of consciousness.* Boulder, CO: Sentient Publications.

Wapnick, K. (1980). Faith and forgiveness in psychotherapy. *Voices: The art and science of psychotherapy.* 16(1). 47-53. In print.

Wapnick, K. (2006). Hearing the melody: The silence of psychotherapy. In Wapnick, G. (Ed.), *A symphony of love: Selections of Dr. Kenneth Wapnick's writings: autobiographies, poetry, short stories, and articles.* (pp. 413-422). Temecula, CA: Foundation for A Course in Miracles.

Wapnick, G. (Ed.) (2016). *A symphony of love: Selections of Dr. Kenneth Wapnick's writings: autobiographies, poetry, short stories, and articles.* Temecula, CA: Foundation for A Course in Miracles.

From the Archives

Spring, 2006

Kenneth Wapnick

KENNETH WAPNICK, PHD is a clinical psychologist who has been working with *A Course in Miracles* since 1973. An integration of spirituality and psychotherapy, the Course is an inspired set of three books that teaches that the way to remember God is by undoing guilt through forgiving others. Ken is President and cofounder, with his wife Gloria, of the *Foundation for A Course in Miracles* in Temecula, California.

Hearing the Melody:
The Silence of Psychotherapy

Introduction

I REMEMBER SITTING IN PAUL FRISCH'S CLASS AT ADELPHI UNIVERSITY IN THE 1960S, LISTENING TO A TAPE HE HAD MADE OF ONE OF HIS THERAPY SESSIONS. Paul was one of the pioneers of the American Academy of Psychotherapists and a dynamic example for us fledgling therapists—his early death was a great loss to us all. As I sat enthralled, I lost all sense of time and space and felt I was listening to a piece of music under the baton of a master conductor. I remember exclaiming afterwards—whether to myself or to Paul—"This is a symphony, not psychotherapy!" As Paul gently guided his patient through his tale of marital woe—periodically punctuating his conducting with the theme: "Do you love her?"—I began to realize the nature of healing. On a level I was not truly in touch with, I knew that regardless of any external shift that may or may not have occurred in the session, healing was present as therapist and patient became one, with the words being mere vehicles to express this non-verbal underground stream of healing.

It was not surprising that listening to Paul's tape would have elicited a musical response from me. For many years, music had been my life's inspiration, with Beethoven specifically in the role of spiritual teacher and guide. Three years after listening to Paul's therapy session, while an intern, I became more conscious of my attempts to integrate this underlying experience—deeply and personally—of a non-verbal flow within and between people. I had returned one evening from a concert of Beethoven's Late Quartets and had been particularly affected by his 14th quartet in c# minor, perhaps the acme of all artistic achievement, having the potential to open one to a trans-human level of experience. I was determined to generalize that experience to the practice of psychotherapy. As I drove the following morning to the clinic for a therapy appointment, wanting to have this "Beethoven experience" become more a part of my life, I vowed that I would try to take my previous evening's listening and make it integral to the session. While I probably got an A for effort, I doubt if my attempts were very successful at integrating the trans-mundane love, which I knew to be the only truth, with my practice of psychotherapy.

However, I was certainly beginning to understand better what Paul Frisch was striving for—in himself and in his students—and knew that such integration was the only meaningful goal, not just for psychotherapy, but for everything I was to do in my life. It was not until many years later, however, when I saw *A Course in Miracles* that I found the perfect guide for this integration. But that is for another article, perhaps. In what follows, I would like to explore the experience of healing from the perspective of both therapist and patient, using music as a metaphor.

Learning to Listen

It has been said that music is the queen of the arts, and great musicians have observed that "What is best in music is not found in the notes" (Gustav Mahler); the conductor should listen to the music "behind the notes" (Wilhelm Furtwangler); and the true music is in the "silence between the notes" (Isaac Stern). Richard Wagner, moreover, urged conductors to listen for the work's melos, the Greek word for "melody," by which he meant the inner melody or soul of the composition, without which the music itself—the notes—would be conducted "without a shadow of soul or sense." In other words, these musicians were stressing the importance of hearing the content of the music, not its form. Similarly, as therapists, we want to hear the underlying call for help and love that masquerades as symptoms, so that we would come to recognize that healing is what comes between the words, however brilliant or insightful our utterances may be. If we are not in touch with the underlying melos of our patients, psychotherapy would be without a shadow of soul or sense.

The great twentieth-century German poet Rilke sets the therapeutic stage for us in this excerpt from his French poem "Gong":

We must close our eyes, renounce our mouths,
remain mute, blind, and dazzled:
with space utterly shaken, what touches us
wants no more from our being than attention.

Yet something interferes with our attention, preventing us from truly listening to our patients and ourselves.

Our point of departure is that it is impossible to hear others as long as we have a need from them that demands to be met. The reason is obvious. Our pressing needs demand satisfaction, regardless of external circumstances. The proper social upbringing we were all exposed to usually allows us to delay such gratification, yet not without a sense of sacrifice. Our unconscious needs ensure that whatever relationships we are in at the moment will be experienced in an adversarial way, whatever their form and however unconscious such perceptions may be. Once others are perceived as necessary for our happiness, peace, or enhanced self-concept, let alone our financial security, they can only be experienced as enemies who deny us what we need, there to be conquered so the fruits of battle can be ours. Either way, we cannot be truly present to others, but only to what our needs make of them.

Following the dictates of our perceived lacks and deprivations, therefore, we seek to find satisfaction for our needs, regardless of the cost, though we hope it will be another who will pay, literally and figuratively. Thus we seek to sacrifice another's happiness in order to find the satisfaction we crave. How, then, can we be present to another? How, then, can we hear the plaintive call for release from pain? How, then, can we find in another the echo of our own call for release? These questions beg for answers if we are to hear truth's answer: we all, in the depths of our being, experience the searing pain of love's absence. The world's overriding concept of self-interest becomes the clarion call of all people—both as individuals and collectively as religious, social, racial, and national groups. Preserving our identity is the goal, and others are inevitably seen as abetting us in our search or thwarting us. Either way, they are not perceived for who they are, but for the purpose that they serve in our quest for self-preservation.

Yet in the silence of truth's oneness, we hear the answer: hearing another's call as our own echoes the truth beyond all seemingly disparate life. This premise of fundamental unity underlies, for example, the core teaching of Buddhism: *compassion for all sentient beings.* Beyond distinctions made between right and wrong, good and evil, mental health or mental illness, rests the simple truth, in the words of Harry Stack Sullivan: *We are all more human than otherwise.* This commonality of human existence is the suffering we share, and it is the pain inherent in life here to which we seek to pay attention. We return to our musical metaphor and the thought that we should listen to the content of the music behind its *form.* This allows our attention to move beyond the pettiness of our judgments and misperceptions to the underlying *content* of love's truth sounding in each of us. Most therapists are familiar with Theodore Reik's wonderful example of listening in his classic work *Listening with the Third Ear,* where he relates the story of a patient who came to his office for her regular appointment. She commented to Reik on a book that was upside down in his bookcase. Without anything else being said, the famed analyst asked: "Why didn't you tell me you had an abortion?" Reik's question, of course, was right on the money, and his book explains how he had derived his surprising conclusion from the woman's comment. The point is not that we necessarily become as shrewdly insightful as the famed psychoanalyst, who Freud considered to be among his most brilliant pupils, but it is important that we listen with the "third ear," freed only when we suspend our need to evaluate situations and judge others—all based on our own perceived needs and pressing personal concerns, however unconscious these may be.

It is a psychotherapeutic axiom that one cannot understand when one judges; judgment being the shadowy projection of separation that keeps people apart, while understanding reflects the light of true communication that binds us together, the etymological meaning, incidentally, of the word *religion.* Thus, learning to listen means learning to give up judgment. This allows us as therapists to listen to our patients, hearing the call to be proven wrong about their preconceptions of their problems and, indeed, their very selves. In releasing the barriers of judgment that hinder communication, the belief in separate interests is undone. The forms of the problem are seen through to the single content of separating and separate interests, and healing occurs as therapists mirror to the patient the shared interests of oneness: hearing the forgotten melody and remembering the love that is their true and shared Self.

In sum, as long as we relate to another out of personal need, judgment is inevitable. Our separate interests become the reality, breeding the demand that these needs be met, always at the expense of another. The therapeutic relationship now exists solely to satisfy these demands, and it becomes the ego's temple at whose shrine we come with our offerings of judgment. The other person has disappeared behind the clouds of scarcity and deprivation, and we no longer truly see or hear. Without these thoughts of separation, however, one can only listen, without imposing one's needs and selfish demands for satisfaction. One is still, quietly doing nothing but being without judgment. As *A Course in Miracles* says about forgiveness:

> Forgiveness...is still, and quietly does nothing...It merely looks, and waits, and judges not (p. 401).

Two Songs

What exactly is it that asks for our attention? one of two songs: love's reflection, or the call for it. Either way, our response is still love. This is an important point, for it allows us to see everything that people do—the good and the bad, the loving and hateful—as falling into one of these two categories. Our natural state is love, wherein we recognize the mutual interests that unites, in a common purpose, all humanity without exception. That alone is the truth in a world that cries out for selfishness and triumph. Yet our pressing need for special uniqueness and self-centered adherence to our desire for supremacy over others seems to far overshadow this innate love that would join us as one. Simply stated, we have become afraid of this oneness, for a little voice whispers incessantly that this way madness lies, echoing King Lear's injunction to himself—we will lose our identity without the means for self-preservation: judgment, attack, and using others to meet our needs. It is this need to be something important, rather than just simply being, that preludes our acceptance of another.

How, then, do we look at judgment—ours or others'? If we see our attacks on another as coming from our fear of love, then these attacks are only defenses, regardless of the form they take. After all, no one in the presence of the love within could ever attack someone else. It would be impossible. Therefore, we can conclude that anyone attacking does not feel this love inside. Yet if that love is truly there, as it must be in everyone—*We are all more human than otherwise*—then it must be the fear of this love that drives us to defend against it by attacking others—blatantly or subtly: in thought, word, or deed. Thus do we all—therapist and patient alike—suffer from the same neurosis of fear, defending against it by ensuring that we remain separated, forever protected against love's encroachment.

Yet when the doors of our perception are cleansed, it will be this fear of love we can know—in ourselves and in our patients. And all we need do to hear this universal call is listen: to be still and hear the cry behind the words, see the despair of hopelessness beyond the symptoms. Our personal and professional belief systems are ultimately irrelevant to this new vision, for they are but the vehicles we use to convey the underlying response of love. And so, to hear these songs of love or fear, and only these, we need to be quiet within, to come without needs unto our patients. In that inner silence, we recognize that we all have these same two melodies running through our minds, determining what we think, feel, and do.

The first of these, again, is love and healing, and the second is the fear of love and healing. The latter is what we typically call *resistance*, and in the end, it is this for which we listen. Once heard, we simply touch it with gentle hands, and its hardness softens and dissolves in a duet of healing whereby two disparate voices—therapist and patient—blend together and sound as one. Resistance never responds to analysis or

Hearing the Melody: The Silence of Psychotherapy   **71**

judgment, but only to the kind reminder that love is unaffected by fear, and so the need to resist it is pointless, if not futile. Thus the therapist must wait patiently, but true patience is born of the certainty of outcome. It is when therapists are able to remind themselves that love waits quietly beyond the clouds of guilt, fear, and attack, and all they need do is be that presence of quiet patience, that healing occurs. They indeed do nothing but be still.

And in that silence, beyond the neediness that distorts perception, we come to understand that what appears to be pathology is only a special form of fear, the same fear of love that cowers in each of us. Yet in the presence of the soundless song of love, the discordant noise of separate and selfish identities must fade and disappear. To the extent we believe in this identity, we shall fear the melody of forgiveness that recalls to mind— literally—the song our true self still sings to all who cross our path, and whom we had heretofore sought to exclude from love, as we sought to exclude ourselves.

When we recognize we have been listening to the wrong song, it is time to truly listen. We then hear our patients' call for help behind the shadows of dissonance, and recognize the call for light that is our own as well. The fog of judgment has no power to conceal the resplendent light of our oneness. When we recognize in people's attacks the desperate call for help; when we hear in their viciousness the underlying pain, how could we not seek to reach out and touch the source of such pain with the gentle hands of forgiveness, knowing it would be our own chains of guilt that would fall away, along with another's? As Prospero, Shakespeare's final hero, says near the end of *The Tempest:*

> Though with their high wrongs I am struck to the quick.
> Yet, with my nobler reason, 'gainst my fury
> Do I take part. The rarer action is
> In virtue than in vengeance. (V,i)

Thus we strive to take the "rarer action" of listening instead of judging, hearing instead of attacking. What had heretofore been conceived in guilt and fear becomes transformed into harmonies of love and healing; the cacophonous world of hate having given way to the sweet sounds of music; the melody of love we sing first to each other metamorphoses as the eternal song we have always sung as spirit. And thus our classroom of relationships radiates the star-lit temple of our and our brothers' mutual healing. Psychotherapy: Purpose, Process, Practice, a companion pamphlet to *A Course in Miracles,* describes the therapist's office in these inspiring words:

> Think what the joining of two brothers really means. And then forget the world and all its little triumphs and its dreams of death. The same are one, and nothing now can be remembered of the world of guilt. The room becomes a temple, and the street a stream of stars that brushes lightly past all sickly dreams (p. 18).

Stated another way, as we help our patients become integrated within themselves, as we become integrated within ourselves, we are also helping to integrate ourselves with our patients: joining undoing separation; shared interests replacing separate interests. The core of psychotherapy, therefore, is therapists first being able to hear their own melody, for only then can they be free to hear their patients'. And in that instant of shining silence, healing is born.

Conclusion: An Invitation to Healing

Our focus, therefore, should not really be on our patients, but on ourselves. It is only arrogance to believe—regardless of our many years of training and experience—that we know what is best for them. Yet there is a wisdom within each of us that does know. Call it intuition, a simple hunch, or the Holy Spirit, an ego-less presence of love dwells in everyone. It is this presence that heals—therapist and patient. Psychotherapy, then, is an invitation for the patient to join the therapist—love calling to love, to be its gift of oneness. Jon Vickers, one of the great tenors of an earlier generation, shared in an interview his thoughts about the gift of his wonderful vocal instrument:

> I am humble before the gift that was given to me....And it was a gift. I have a great sense of gratitude toward the giver of that gift. I can't stand it when people think what they have was given to themselves. Whether you're Albert Einstein or Placido Domingo, be grateful, use it, give it to your audience....The gift that I gave to an audience—and I was very blessed in that I had the power to do it—[was to] reach my arms through the proscenium arch to pull the audience in, to embrace them, to say to them: "Come up here with me. Know these feelings, and you will have the reward of experiencing the absolute beauty of *Fidelio*, the greatness of the tragedy of *Othello*. Come up here. Share it with me" (*New York Times*, Nov. 19, 2000, Arts & Leisure section).

Vickers was speaking of great artists—including in that category creative geniuses— but we can adapt his thoughts to what we can be as psychotherapists. Accepting the gift of love from within, it can only extend through us, its non-specific content taking whatever form is most helpful to our patients, as it invites them to share it with us. Our role as therapists is to strive to truly hear, so that love's truth can meet our patients' needs in the specific form in which it can be accepted without fear. Thus it is not the type of psychotherapy we do, and hopefully our theoretical orientation is flexible, but the egoless love with which we do it. Our prayer to ourselves as therapists, therefore, should echo Lorenzo's words to Jessica in *The Merchant of Venice*, which bespeak what could be the harmony of all our relationships, professional and personal alike, if we so choose:

> Here will we sit, and let the sounds of music
> Creep in our ears: soft stillness and the night
> Become the touches of sweet harmony. (V,i)

What, then, should be our challenge as psychotherapists other than to allow the inner conductor to mold our instrument, that it bespeaks truth's soft stillness? What else would we desire for ourselves and for our patients? What, in the end, is psychotherapy but the sweet harmony in which therapist and patient begin as two individuals, and ultimately blend their voices into the sounds of love's healing music—the melody of gentle silence?   ▼

REFERENCES

A Course in Miracles: Text, Workbook for Students, Manual for Teachers. (1976). Belvedere: CA: Foundation for Inner Peace.

Psychotherapy: Purpose, process and practice. (1976). Belvedere, CA: Foundation for Inner Peace.

William Boylin

WILLIAM BOYLIN practiced in psychiatric hospitals for over 33 years and is currently in private practice in Middlefield, Connecticut. He is adjunct faculty at Central Connecticut State University. For 10 years he coordinated a family therapy consultation group with Carl Whitaker, MD. He is the author of *Bedlam*, a novel about a psychiatric hospital, as well as numerous journal articles and his professional blog at williamboylin.com.
wboylin@aol.com

Ambushed

IT WAS A SATURDAY MORNING WHEN MY BROTHER CALLED INVITING ME TO A WORKSHOP IN WHICH HE WAS PARTICIPATING. In the spring of 1977, the Gestalt Institute of Connecticut was hosting Carl Whitaker for the weekend. Monthly, they invited the gurus of psychotherapy from around the country for workshops. Considering this a great opportunity, I jumped in my car and flew to the meeting. They were still on a break when I arrived. My brother took me around to meet everyone. I already knew a number of the clinicians, including having previously met Carl.

Shortly, everyone settled down and the meeting convened. I found a couple of pillows next to my brother. When it was quiet for a minute, one of the men started thanking Carl for working with his family last year. The work had resulted in greater connectedness and joy within the family. I felt honored to be watching this.

Following another short silence, my brother spoke up: "Carl, about 6 months ago, our mother was killed. At the time, I was close to my brother, but we're not close any more and I want to improve our relationship." Every eye turned to me.

I was totally taken by surprise. This I did not expect. I didn't know what to do. Then Carl extended the invitation, "Would you like to work on this?" In my wildest dreams I wouldn't have known how to say no. "Sure."

Several things then happened at once. I literally could feel all the people sitting around me very slowly moving away. The next thing I was aware of was one of the psychiatrists turning on the video camera. What made this all tolerable was that Carl came over and sat down on a pillow next to us. We were now a threesome sitting alone in front of the camera and a room full of people.

Carl Whitaker was an intimidating presence. A big strong farm boy who had left the dairy farm for a professional career, he was tall and broad, an imposing personal stature. However, I must emphasize his kindliness and his brilliant mind. I felt safe with him next to me.

For the next 2 hours, Carl went up one side of my family tree and down the other. He explored deep family themes. My brother and I talked about the loneliness we each felt. We talked about the horror of our mother's murder. We both cried repeatedly.

After the session, I could not have told you one specific thing we said. Over the years, I have come to understand this. Carl talked in such a basic, primitive language, that he kept pushing us into the unconscious side of the brain. He talked primary process and my brain followed him into the depths of my unconscious. It wasn't that we just talked about the love for our mother that we had when we were 3 or 4; we *felt* the love for our mother that we had when we were 3 or 4. Being that we were talking from the depths of our psyche, my mind wasn't holding on to what was said.

I do remember how it ended. After lovingly exploring our family for 2 hours, Carl leaned back and gave a big laugh. He then held out his two big arms as if he were holding two babies: "I feel like I have each of you on a different breast and I can't get you together." Then he laughed. He wrapped his hands behind each of our necks and pulled us together.

As soon as we touched, we were hugging and sobbing. We were now two little boys who had lost their mother. We held onto each other and sobbed for a few minutes before the moment ebbed. My brother sat back and looked at me: "You know that now we're both orphans?"

Carl then spoke: "I want you both to leave, walk on the beach, hold hands, throw sand at each other. We're going to talk about what just happened and I don't want our talking to alter what you just experienced, so you have to leave." We slowly wandered out to the sand and walked and talked.

What happened over the next few months was extraordinary. As I went through my grieving and my attempts to avoid my grief, whenever I came to a roadblock, I would remember something that we had talked about. It was as if Carl had scattered breadcrumbs all through my unconscious. As I stepped on one, a memory would come back that would be like a new piece of the puzzle, that would help me make sense of who I was and what losing my mother really meant.

In 1982, I was working in an adolescent psychiatric hospital with another veteran of Elmcrest Psychiatric Institute who shared my appreciation of Carl. One day he asked me if I thought Carl really did offer supervision to people like us. I suggested we ask him. The next thing I knew, he had Carl on the phone and he wanted to know when we would begin supervision. I was totally surprised, but we set an appointment.

Carl later told me that it was during the session with my brother that I captured him as a foster-grandfather. Through 10 years of supervision, he nurtured me. He shared what he thought psychotherapy was, but he talked much more about what it meant to be a person, a husband, and a father. He encouraged me to look inside and work on my own growth. I will forever be appreciative of this gift. ▼

Penelope Norton

PENELOPE NORTON, PHD, practices psychology in Ormond Beach, Florida. She provides psychotherapy to children, teens, adults, couples, families and seniors. Her 35 years of practice have brought her increasing confidence and humility. She is inspired by Ralph Waldo Emerson, who wrote, "What lies behind us and what lies before us are tiny matters compared to what lies within us."
psynorton@aol.com

Editor's note: This article and the four that follow are adapted from Dana Jack's plenary presentation and three panelists at AAP's 2018 Institute & Conference in Atlanta.

Introduction of Dana Jack

IN THE EARLY 1990S, THREE ELEMENTS OF MY EXPERIENTIAL LIFE BRAIDED TOGETHER, FORCING ME TO CONFRONT A NEW PARADIGM. Having studied developmental psychology, I had assimilated these experiences, but their convergence forced accommodation. That is, I had to change an aspect of my model of the world.

The first of the experiences occurred on a very warm Mother's Day in 1956, when, fortunately, we were having dinner with my grandparents, who lived a few miles from our home. While we were at my grandparents', a powerful (some say F4) tornado hit our home and neighborhood.

Late in the day, we rode in my grandparents' Chevy to inspect the damage. I was in the back, in my grandmother's lap. The police blocked access to the area, but with the help of my parents' driver's licenses and ID, we were able to proceed. As we drove up I saw pieces of bright red twisted metal strewn in a nearby field. I do not remember anyone getting out of the car (though they did) or seeing the house (though I must have), but I DO remember saying with distress, "That's my new swing set!" My grandmother said, "SH! Sh! Sh! No, it's not! Sh! Sh! Sh!" That was the beginning, as I remember it, of many years of silencing, especially at times when my words or self-expression might be at odds with others' needs. I have written about the tornado elsewhere (Norton, 2001), but suffice it to say, our house had major damage, and we lived with my grandparents for quite a time after that.

Second, in 1990, on a cold, dark December night, I rode through a remote part of the Ocala National Forest, my husband at the wheel, my 3-year-old and my 10-month-old in the back seat of our old Volvo. We were going about 70 miles per hour when SMACK we hit a deer. With the impact, the hood of the car flew over the windshield. We couldn't see where we were going. I screamed my terror, opened my mouth, and *no sound came out*. I was open-mouthed, full-throated, and SILENT! Unbelievable! My power failed me. The experience and shock of my loss of voice anchored me to silence's capacity to handicap.

The third experience was less dramatic, but still significant to my change in paradigm. By the time of the deer incident, I had been practicing psychology for about 8-10 years. I was moving inexorably away from what I perceived as the depersonalizing judgment of psychological testing and was focusing on psychotherapy. In my practice, I was a daily witness to the loss of voice of so many clients, especially those with trauma histories. I began to see two elements of voicelessness: the physiological loss of voice that occurs during trauma (akin to classical conditioning), and the behavioral loss of voice (akin to operant conditioning) by others' demands for silence. I think of this second form of voicelessness as *learned voicelessness*. And, this demand for silence falls disproportionately on children, women, racial and cultural minorities.

After the convergence of these experiences, I happened across Dana Jack's first book, *Silencing the Self: Women and Depression* (1991). It was, in an expression given me by one of my clients, a "paper mirror." It spoke what I had not been able to integrate, personally or professionally. I began using Jack's Silencing the Self Scale with clients in a new testing paradigm, collaborative assessment. I became more attuned to the ways in which I had been silenced, and continued to be silenced. I also became much more attuned to the ways in which clients had been disempowered by lack of voice, and better able to help them reclaim both voice and self-efficacy.

By the late '90s, we had added a daughter to our family, and encouraging her voice became an important part of my relationship with her. I was so proud of her first book, published when she was in second grade, entitled, *The Princess Who Told Her Tale*.

Not long after this, I joined the Academy, began writing for *Voices*, and a few years later still became co-editor of *Voices* with Doris Jackson. The first person I wanted to introduce to the Academy through the journal was Dana Jack, which I did with an interview of her and an article by her in 2010.

From further study of Jack's second, prizewinning book *Silencing the Self Across Cultures* (2010), I received still more personal and professional validation of the multicultural nature of self-silencing, which continues to influence my thought and work. The power of this paradigm is everywhere, now that I have been alerted to its presence: In her wonderful 2018 memoir, Clemantine Wamariya describes the moment when she had to flee the Rwandan massacre: "We heard a knock on the door. My grandmother gestured for us to be silent—checkeka checkeka checkeka" (p. 25).

In continuing this thread of awareness, I am honored to be included with Dr. Jack in this series of articles on self-silencing for *Voices*. ▼

References

Jack, D. (1991). *Silencing the self: Women and depression.* New York: Harper Collins.

Jack, D. and Ali, A. (2010.) *Silencing the self across cultures: Depression and gender in the social world.* Oxford, England: Oxford University Press.

Norton, P. (2001). Braiding the fringe. *Voices: The art and science of psychotherapy*, 2001, 37:1, 58-62.

Wamariya, C. and Weil, E. (2018). *The girl who smiled beads: A story of war and what comes after.* New York: Crown Publishers.

Dana Jack

Silence Sounds

DANA C. JACK, EdD, professor emerita, Fairhaven College of Interdisciplinary Studies/Western Washington University, earned her BA at Mount Holyoke College, MSW at University of Washington, and EdD at Harvard University. She authored the Silencing the Self Scale and theory. Her four books have been translated into numerous languages; she received APA's International Division book award (2012) for *Silencing the Self Across Cultures* (co-editor Alisha Ali). Jack was a therapist for seven years prior to her doctoral studies.
dana.jack@wwu.edu
https://works.bepress.com/dana_jack/

Whatever you have to say, leave
The roots on, let them
Dangle
And the dirt
Just to make clear
Where they come from.

—Charles Olson (1987)

I HAVE BEEN INTRIGUED BY SILENCE MY WHOLE LIFE. I was four when first I heard silence. It is one of my strongest early memories. I was sitting upstairs, alone; others in the house were quiet. There was an absence of noise—but it wasn't quiet. I perceived a sound, a thrumming—almost like a vibration that was within me and surrounded me. Not knowing what it was, I asked my mother. She dismissed the question.

From then on, I occasionally heard this puzzling sound of silence: walking alone in the fields of South Texas; waiting in the stillness of early morning for the rural school bus; going to sleep. And other times. I was told something was wrong with my hearing, though nothing was.

As an adult, I learned the Buddhist teaching that when the mind is open and relaxed, we can hear this sound of silence, which some call a cosmic hum. They say that silence can be heard even in the midst of loud noise, like traffic, chainsaws, or an argument. They say that if we learn to detect, embrace, and tune into the sound of silence, we can keep one foot in the well of stillness that lies beyond the pull of immediate circumstances. We can stay with ourselves in harmony. We can learn to respond and not react to strong emotional triggers.

This positive well of internal silence is full of calm, empty of self-absorption. In this quiet stillness, we may begin to hear the ineffable. External circumstances can help foster this experience. When I walk through the forest in back of our house, it is quiet, yet brimming with the fullness of life. Raven caw and wren trill pierce the air, filling the space with vocalizations that speak to us beyond words. It is easy to feel connected to the deep innerness of all things in this positive silence.

On the other hand, as a child I learned that silence can be negative. Because of an alcoholic, violent father, I often retreated to silence as self-protection, seeking safe hiding places and learning not to express my own feelings. Exposure carried danger. I experienced how concealing myself led to a place of isolation, immobilization and depression where I was filled with fear, anger, and shame.

During the late 1950s, my parents divorced and my mother sank into a major depression, blaming herself for the failure of her marriage. She often wept, trying to understand what had happened and asking herself, "What have I done wrong?" As a child, I wanted to understand. I also felt a strong sense of unfairness over her predicament as the woman who was "left behind," who went to work at a low-paying job while my father continued his high-income, fast lifestyle. Living in Texas where male dominance was unquestioned, my mother had no sense of the structures that shaped her and through which she evaluated her worth.

Even though I was young, I knew that my mother was trapped in a false view of herself. She never got angry about the unfairness; she never said what she thought and felt; she retreated into silence and her own alcoholism. Although my mother was courageous, caring for three children by herself while working outside the home, she felt emptied of value. What was this about? The pain of her depression, the unfairness that elevated men's possibilities while curtailing women's, and a desire to comprehend the complexity of what happened led to my lifelong quest to investigate silence and depression. Not only that, it also led to my struggles with coming to voice.

What Is Silencing the Self?

I am so distant from the hope of myself,
in which I have goodness, and discernment...
—Mary Oliver, "When I Am Among the Trees"

Listening to silence has played a critical role in understanding and formulating the theory and measurement of silencing the self. Three defining points stand out.

The first was noticing the absence of descriptions about women's experience of depression from their own point of view. While working as a therapist in a university counseling center for 7 years, I mostly saw depressed young women who talked about their unsatisfactory relationships, low self-esteem, and thwarted sense of self. I read everything available on women's depression in the 1970s, only to learn that they were described as "dependent," hanging onto relationships like "leeches," and failures at developing autonomy.

I headed back to Harvard for doctoral studies with a passion to do my dissertation on women's depression. As part of the research, I interviewed 12 clinically depressed women in a longitudinal exploration, starting with the question, "What do you think led up to your depression?" I will never forget poring over their transcribed interviews, feeling that capturing their experience lay just beyond my understanding. It rested in the hollows, pools and absences of their words. Yet, as sounds of water are amplified by the

Silence Sounds   **79**

dips and eddies in a stream, so were their words intensified by my resonance with them. My story ran through theirs like water, sometimes merging with theirs to mingle, other times tracing a different course to reveal where we fell into cracks, slipped underground to become trapped. Listening required putting an ear to what seemed inaudible, transforming it into meaning. It meant attending to the women's silences, and to my own.

Through the process of listening to common themes among all the women, the phenomenon I named "silencing the self" became clear. The women described how certain images of relatedness—"oneness," "self-sacrificing," "pleasing"—directed them to silence vital aspects of self out of fear that voicing them would threaten their relationships or their safety. Seeing and judging themselves through others' eyes increased their self-restriction. Silencing their voices led to a fall in self-esteem and what they described as a "loss of self." It was clear that *voice* did not mean only the literal act of speaking but referred to their ability to reveal and affirm in relationships core parts of themselves that felt central to their identity.

Because we are relational beings, expressing our feelings and thoughts to others is part of creating, deepening and/or changing ourselves and the quality of our relationships. Though the goals of self-silencing are to protect the self and avoid loss, the sad irony is that pursuing these aims through suppressing oneself leads to the opposite— to a "loss of self" *and* the loss of authentic, satisfactory relationship. Removing central pieces of ourselves from interaction eliminates any possibility of real mutuality, which is founded on honest, open dialogue.

Self-silencing leads to self-alienation and a feeling of being lost to oneself. Pretending "I will be what (I think) you need me to be" to gain love and safety makes it easy to believe the enactment and eventually, grow unable to know which feelings are true. What is real—the silenced self or the false self, designed to please others and avoid conflict? Especially when others are responding to the pleasing façade, we can wonder if they really like *us*, and also question if the relationship is real or artificial. Abandoning one's self in this way can cause deep anger and inner division; interacting with others can feel like a manipulation to achieve specific goals. In this broader sense, self-silencing means denying one's authentic self—one's creativity, ambition, sexuality, and many other deepest aspects of self that push for expression. It means hiding.

The second defining point was recognizing how culture is largely silent about the power dynamics that influence our society and our inner worlds. Those who are less powerful, primarily women, cultural, racial and sexual minorities, are often shamed and punished for speaking or acting against the inequality and repression they experience. In the words of women who were depressed, I heard how their small, everyday interactions were shaped by the larger power structures played out within intimate relationships. Often, women have had to choose silence because it is the least harmful of a number of difficult choices. Some men, too, self-silence with devastating consequences, but from different motivations and with different consequences. Hiding vulnerability through editing one's words, feelings and actions in compliance with demands of "masculinity" is associated with men's depression. Yet it also protects and reproduces men's position of dominance through their appearance of strength and through the reality of their social position.

A third defining point came with transforming what I heard in the women's narratives into a research instrument. In order to determine whether depression was associated with retreating into silence, pleasing others, interacting from a false self and sacrificing oneself, it was clear that the construct of self-silencing had to be measurable and quantifiable.

The result was the Silencing the Self Scale (STSS), comprised of sentences and/or concepts that reflected depressed women's beliefs about how to make and maintain their relationships (Jack & Dill, 1992). Using this scale, over 130 peer-reviewed, published studies and researchers from 30 countries have investigated how self-silencing associates with and predicts depression and other negative psychological and health effects (see Researchers List under https://works.bepress.com/dana_jack/). The studies demonstrate that the negative effects of self-silencing cross cultural lines as well as geographical boundaries.

Because the cognitive schemas measured by the STSS are relational and also phenomenological (reflecting the experience of a divided self when one self-silences), I thought they could provide a basis for individual and group therapy (see Jack, 1991, 1999b; Jack & Ali, 2010). Currently, other researchers are developing models of intervention based on overcoming self-silencing—for example, with eating disorders and HIV/AIDS (see Jack & Ali, 2010).

What are the mechanisms by which self-silencing leads to depression and other negative effects? We know that depression's origins are multi-causal, influenced by multiple interacting pathways among psychological processes, physiology, and the familial and cultural worlds. Since the STSS was published, there has been an unparalleled convergence of neuroscience, evolutionary theory, and psychology that affirms the importance of positive relationships to human functioning. The brain itself is a social organ; its very structure and biology are shaped by social contexts and interpersonal interactions throughout life. These contexts affect the body/mind not only through neurochemical responses but also by assigning meaning to physical events and social interactions. Self-silencing negates the self, disrupts connection, and leads to isolation and self-alienation. It appears that silencing the self interacts with a range of processes known to precipitate depression, such as a negative experience of self, a threat of separation that in turn engages the attachment system, and an activation of neurobiological systems and higher order self-regulatory cognitions. Because relational disconnection constitutes a major threat to the self, self-silencing appears to be a crucial element in precipitating depression.

How Does Self-Silencing Relate to the Practice of Therapy?

Because of early childhood experiences, I have found it difficult to say what I'm feeling, especially when fearing it may lead to shame or harm relationships. In therapy, this meant that my words carried shadows of things unsaid, of omissions, of fears. Through listening, therapists who are attuned to the silence beyond words can coax the shadows between and surrounding the words to reveal themselves. But only with one therapist did this happen for me. With others, I remained hidden. I did not stay with these therapists, nor benefit from the meetings we did have. Such experiences, inadvertently, increased the conviction that certain things could not be spoken about. I'm sure these therapists were well-intentioned and probably not avoiding my areas of self-silencing; often our clients are very skilled at hiding.

Silence Sounds

As a therapist, I, too, self-silenced. After my MSW and before pursuing a doctorate, I practiced for 7 years at a university counseling center. Through that experience, I learned that the areas in which I self-silenced with clients were those I avoided because they were too painful or frightening. One young man, tall, seemingly self-possessed and confident, came in because of depression. On his second visit, he described his experience of self as "pure emptiness." "There's nothing there," he said, "I don't really exist." His descriptions of childhood were flat, unremarkable, devoid of emotion. Not really knowing how to help him, feeling caught and made somewhat anxious by his description, I referred him to a colleague who worked with men. But, honestly, I did so while suppressing the painful and confusing emotions stirred up by his account. Not until after my own extensive therapy did I realize that such reactions came from my background of abusive, alcoholic parents who required that I take care of them. In part, I didn't exist; I had no substance. At least I had the self-awareness to refer this client elsewhere. But the issue stands. We self-silence as therapists when the client brings us our own unresolved issues, our fear of the pain their explorations will cause us. It took years to be with and bear the ache of my personal history.

So how do we create a space in which our clients feel free to speak their shame, fear, experiences of transference—their forbidden feelings? It happens, in part, through listening for what lies behind the client's words, and for what we selectively exclude from expression in ourselves. The therapist's creation of a warm, welcoming place of transformation that *includes* silence is important. But not the silence of the therapist's own unexplored, shame-filled aspects of self or unresolved traumas. Rather, the comfortable silence of the therapist's self-knowledge and self-acceptance that allows *being with* the client. This silence is one of stillness of mind, of openness, without preconceptions that he or she knows who this person is, what they need to explore, what they might say. The positive well of silence is a container that can offer acceptance and safety.

Many have written of this mysterious terrain of being with the client in chosen moments of silence. For example, Mark Epstein (1996) says,

> Psychotherapy requires a silence that permits a patient to act out whatever she is otherwise out of touch with, or to say what she is otherwise out of touch with, or to say what she has not previously allowed herself to think. We are all hungry for this kind of silence, for it is what allows us to repossess those qualities from which we are estranged (p. 187).

In my own experience as a client, the one therapist who gave permission for alienated, traumatized parts of myself to speak provided safety though his state of mind, a state of mind that silently communicated he was fully present. That his mind was not preoccupied with himself or his own thoughts. That his mind rested in a still openness and receptivity that was trustworthy. And that nothing I said would be judged or disallowed.

This quality of being is hard to describe but is sensed—minds communicate with each other without words. As Dan Siegel (2012) has explained,

> ....even at a physical distance one mind can directly influence the activity... and development of another through the transfer of energy and information. This joining process occurs via both verbal and nonverbal behaviors, which function as signals sent from one mind to another. ...The expression of these emotional elements of social signals serves to activate the very neuronal circuits that mediate the receiver's emotional response: orienting attention, appraising meaning, and creating arousal. ....It is in this manner that the emotional state of the sender directly shapes that of the receiver....Two differentiated individuals can become linked as a part of a resonating whole. This is interpersonal integration (p. 308).

How often do we veer away from silence/stillness when our client might need it? How often do we not listen?

One empathetic, kind woman, when I was sobbing in our second meeting, came to sit next to me on the couch, put her arm around me, and said, "It's okay to cry." This felt like an intrusive caring that had to do with her own needs; it seemed to come from a place that didn't invite exploration of the origins of my pain. Instead, it was foreclosed by comforting. But it felt as if she were comforting herself, that my pain was not something she could bear.

Empathetic alignment is complex territory. As therapists, when is our empathy expressed, and when kept quiet to be sent, as Siegel says, by our own emotional state of resonating empathy? Alternatively, when is our overt communication not based in deep resonance with another person's feeling state, but meant to affect how that person is feeling about *us*? People pleasing, a hallmark of self-silencing, is always about the *self*, imagining how the other person is feeling about *me* and trying to create or manipulate a situation to have it reflect positively on the self. True empathy differs: It's focusing on the other person and the wish to help without the necessity of fulfilling my own needs for affirmation from the client.

When practicing as a therapist, I was too full of my own desire—the desire to help, to be of use—to know what to do with my empathy. This wall of desire could have been sensed by clients; certainly it blocked my ability to be fully present, to hear beyond their words. It also led to an anxiety: Could I help? Was I doing it right? Over time, these anxious desires probably would have lessened had I remained in practice. Instead, I pursued further studies and moved to teaching and research.

Finally, what is this mysterious aspect that we call "coming to voice," and how does it relate to authenticity and to culture? Though we are many possible selves, we can intuit when we are connected to some core aspect of self. It feels like coming home, but to a home much more expansive and potent than the small, egocentric self we usually live in. Staying with this aspect of ourselves allows a positive well of silence out of which authentic speech comes.

We each carry this possibility to know ourselves, who we are, what our interests are, how and what we have to contribute. What emerges from being in alignment with our real self doesn't have to be big or earth-shaking, it simply needs to be unblocked, never silenced. Coming to voice is a lifetime process; we never fully arrive but become more and more able to express ourselves from a place of authenticity. We need to keep the channel open, not biting our tongue or truncating our life. Do we feel free to reveal ourselves to others? To speak up about injustices? Can we share who we are, "leaving the roots on...and the dirt"? Can we live our truths, bring our whole selves into relationships? Or do we hide, putting ourselves aside to earn love and approval and stay safe?

Coming to voice not only requires personal courage, it challenges the culture: the personal is always political. Voice and silence reflect power structures at all levels of relationship—among partners and friends, in the workplace and society—that privilege some voices while excluding others. Speaking ourselves carries consequences that range from positive personal and social change to dangerous and harmful consequences. This has been apparent from the gains, but also the backlash, from the #BlackLivesMatter, #MeToo, and LGBTQ movements. Ideally, we are heard, which means that our voice has

Silence Sounds

reached another, possibly to have an effect. Since silence freezes dialogue and deadens exchange, there is more hope in voicing ourselves than remaining silent with the known negative personal and relational outcomes.

References

Epstein, M. (1996). *Thoughts without a thinker.* New York: Basic Books.

Oliver, M. (2006). When I am among the trees. In *Thirst: Poems* (p. 4). Boston: Beacon Press.

Olson, C. (1987). These days. In George F. Butterick, (Ed). *The collected poems of Charles Olson—excluding Maximus Poems.* Berkeley, CA: University of California Press.

Siegel, D. (2012). *The developing mind: How relationships and the brain interact to shape who we are.* New York: Guilford Press.

A wise man once said nothing.

—Anonymous

How I Speak
Noah Meyers

I STUTTER. THIS IS VERY HARD FOR ME TO SAY. It is hard to say emotionally because it feels shameful, but it is also literally hard to speak this word out loud. Stutter. Putting together these phonemes in this order and speaking this out loud with mouth and tongue is particularly hard for people who stutter, which feels like a cruel twist of fate. Another thing that those of us who stutter have difficulty saying is our names, which is also kind of a bitch. My name is generally difficult for me to say because it's harder to use my tactics of changing my breath or adding in extra words to be able to say it more fluently. When someone asks me my name, it would be hard for me to say, "uhhh........ Noah," without risking being seen as quite a strange person. I almost never remember anyone's name when I first meet them because I am concentrating so hard on saying my name fluently.

For those of us with a stutter, every word or phrase lies on a difficulty-to-pronounce continuum, and we unconsciously scan forward in a sentence so we can employ our little tricks (such as changing a word or adding in extra words or pauses) in order to speak more fluently. I didn't even know that I was doing this until a speech pathologist told me about this phenomenon when I was in high school. I just figured that everyone did it. It's hardest to speak fluently when the listener has clear expectations of what I will be saying, such as when I'm saying my name, but this also extended to saying "hello" when I would answer my house phone growing up, and to reading aloud in class when everyone was following along in their own books.

NOAH MEYERS, PHD, is a clinical psychologist in private practice in Washington, DC. He received his undergraduate degree from Cornell University and his doctorate from American University. Noah has spent much of his life working to un-silence himself in a very literal way, most recently by publishing this in *Voices*.
noahmeyers@gmail.com

Even reading this right now is very hard for me because I can't talk around the hard words. As I've been preparing this talk, I've struggled to write literally every sentence. Should I write down the exact words that I think would best convey what I want to share, or should I tweak the sentence structure or words ever so slightly so that it will be easier for me to say fluently? For example, I strongly considered starting this talk by saying, "I stutter when I speak," which I thought might be easier for me to say fluently than just, "I stutter." Basically, I've been asking myself how important it is to me to say exactly what I want to say, and avoid the strong pull, which is almost always a default, to slightly modify everything that I say so that I can say it fluently. For this talk, I've chosen not to modify or deviate from exactly what I want to say, so I may be stuttering more. Or maybe I'm not. Another hard part is that I never know how my speech will be on any given day or in any given moment. I'm unable to anticipate whether I've spoken these past few paragraphs perfectly fluently or whether I've been stuttering over every other word.

However, if I did choose to modify my sentences, very likely you would not be able to tell. It's easy for me to do, and hard for you to tell. And, thus, maybe you can see how this can be a slippery slope into silencing the self in a quite literal way. It was less about me not speaking my truth than me choosing not to speak for fear of stuttering. This silence could range from what I ordered in a restaurant (if "veggie pizza" was easier to say than "chicken sandwich"); to which classes I signed up to take in college (which certainly did not include any classes with an oral presentation); to pretending that I was sick so that I could stay home from elementary school when I knew that it was my turn to read in class; to not going up to introduce myself to someone I wanted to meet. Some of you who know me today might describe me as an extroverted person, and I think I am, too. But growing up I often remained so quiet you might have confused me for a shy introvert.

As I searched my memory for a clear example to share with you, my thoughts turned to my 8th-grade girlfriend. Her name was Ali, which was a hard word for me to say. We really liked each other a lot, and when I went away to camp for the summer, I promised to call her often. At my camp there was one pay phone near the main office, which the older campers could use in the evenings to call our parents or friends. Once every few nights I would go up to this payphone and call Ali's number. My heart would be beating out of my chest from the fear that one of her parents might answer the phone and I would have to say, "Hi—is Ali there?" Most times I called, one of her parents did pick up the phone. I immediately would be seized with panic, and I would make a split-second decision: Do I ask, "Is Ali home?" and risk stuttering extensively over the word "A-a-a-a-a-ali," or should I just hang up the phone? Three out of four calls, I just hung up. I kind of felt like a creep for repeatedly calling their house and hanging up over the course of the summer, and I buffered my shame slightly by convincing myself that maybe Ali's parents didn't know it was me. The other outcome of these failures was that I didn't get to talk with Ali very often that summer. Even writing about this now evokes that old, strong sense of shame, like an odor that was closely tied to a memory or place but which you haven't smelled in a while. This example of me trying desperately to call my girlfriend over the summer is just one of hundreds of ways that my stutter silenced me and/or evoked my shame when I was growing up.

The worst part of stuttering, of course, is the strong feelings of embarrassment and shame that accompany it. When I was growing up, I was teased by other students for the way that I spoke, and I developed a deep insecurity related to being stupid, unworthy, less-than, and all of the other crappy thoughts and feelings that go along with shame. Just as bad as the teasing from my peers, though, was the reaction of the adults in my life. I still remember the feeling of looking up at an adult while I tried to say something and witnessing the confusion, empathic anxiety, or pity clearly expressed on their face as they looked down at me, waiting for me to finish what I was saying. Often, they tried to guess what I wanted to say and then say the word or phrase for me. Often their guesses were wrong, but sometimes I still went along with it so as not to have to suffer through the rest of my sentence. And what increased my sense of shame even more was that adults would never just *acknowledge* my stutter. In an effort to save my feelings and probably take care of their own anxiety, the adults in my life would pretend it wasn't happening. This, of course, only taught me that stuttering was obviously *so bad* that it just couldn't be acknowledged and had to be moved past as quickly as possible.

When I speak of "adults," I include my parents, aunts and uncles, teachers and babysitters, as well as strangers. Almost nobody was willing to talk about it with me.

This included my father, who had overcome a bad stutter that was present during most of his childhood and young adulthood, and who didn't share this with me until I was in high school. This also included my mother, whose own ever-present anxiety would spike when she felt my anxiety when I stuttered, which only served to increase my anxiety, which worsened my stutter, which increased her anxiety again, and the cycle just continued from there.

My stutter is a physical manifestation of my anxiety, but it's also related to other big feelings that I may be experiencing. While I will still sometimes stutter even when I'm totally at ease, in general, the more anxious I'm feeling, the more I stutter. This anxiety can be either in the moment or during an anxious period in my life. Thus, part of my strategy to control my stutter was to control my feelings, with a particular focus on controlling my anxiety. I've been trying to tamp down and control my feelings for so long now that I can't actually remember when I started or what it was like to have more, bigger feelings. The other complicated piece was that controlling my feelings and pretending I was relaxed and confident actually worked! The more even-keeled I was, the less I stuttered, and then the more calm and confident I felt. This fake-it-'til-you-make-it strategy worked especially well in college, when I was away from my anxious mother and could "rebrand" myself as the social, outgoing kid who was friends with everyone. The paradox was that while I was fostering a long-silenced part of myself and getting more in touch with my extroversion, I was simultaneously creating so much distance between the anxious, stuttering child and the outgoing, social, fluently-speaking adult that I started to lose touch with the part of myself that could feel vulnerable. By being relatively successful at controlling my stutter and finding my voice, I was silencing my anxiety, fear, and vulnerability, which made it harder to connect with myself and with others on a deeper level.

Many people that know me now, even potentially some people in this audience before this talk, don't know that I stutter. When I started to feel secure enough to begin to talk about it with others, I experienced total disbelief when anyone would say they were surprised to learn I have a stutter. At first, I figured that, just like all the adults did when I was growing up, people were pretending not to notice and trying to take care of my feelings when they lied and told me they didn't notice anything different about my speech. But I've now heard it enough times from enough people to believe that some people might actually not notice that I stutter. I'm still taking this on faith, though, because when I stutter now it sounds like a megaphone being directed toward my eardrums, and I experience an almost-physiological reaction of feeling small and ashamed. It takes over my entire body. When I started therapy, my therapist asked me whether I would be willing to stutter again if it meant that I could get most of the other things in my life that I really wanted but did not yet have. My answer at the time was a definitive "NO." But as I've grown, I've realized that my work around my stutter may be less about gaining control over it than accepting it so I can open up to deeper feelings. I still feel some ambivalence about being "ok" if I stutter a lot, but I'm working on it.

As I've been writing this talk, I don't know how much I will stutter when I'm reading it to you all now. Maybe I've stuttered a lot and have had trouble getting through it, or maybe I've been pretty fluent. And I realize, as I'm writing this, that I don't know which one I'll be hoping for. ▼

Kristin Staroba

KRISTIN STAROBA, MSW, has presented and co-led workshops at AAP Summer Workshops, I&Cs, and salons. As editor of this journal, she endeavors to foster writers' voices speaking about our work, and as AAP's new president-elect, she hopes to represent the voice of the membership. Kristin practices in Washington, DC, working with adults in individual, group and couples psychotherapy, and specializes in supervision for newer therapists. *kristin.staroba@gmail.com*

The Road Goes Ever On and On

At a recent dinner for my father's 84th birthday—attended by my parents, my husband and me, and our two college-age sons—I told a story about how pleased I was to be turning a now-unused bedroom into my office at home. I had ripped up the carpet and redone the wood floor, painted the walls a deep pink, and received as a gift from my guys a drafting table for planned art projects. My younger son, himself about to launch and leave for college, took several moments to tell me how glad he was that I had this room to myself; how I did so much for my family and hadn't had my own solo space for years and so deserved this lovely corner of the house. He looked me in the eye the whole time, and I felt tears and a warm sweetness as we connected. Not missing a beat, my mother leaned in between us, trying to engage my eye, "You and I are really alike that way, aren't we? We both love houses!"

This is a picture of how my mother is now: unconsciously making everything about her, missing utterly that the moment was between my son and me, that I might have wanted to respond to him, delight in the glow. I glanced at her and didn't say anything. My son and I exchanged a meaningful wide-eyed look; he nodded slightly, acknowledging that he understood what I would have said had she not upstaged us.

Imagining a revised scene in which I open my mouth to say, "Mom! Hang on and let us have our moment," I can immediately list three reasons I don't.

Why I Silence Myself

One: To hang on to being separate. She can't stand our not being merged or enmeshed, which we were when I was young. I remember crushing homesickness and feeling invisible or insubstantial when away from her (for instance, staying overnight at a friend's when very young, or later at sleep-away camp). She struggles to identify how we are still the same. My parents worked in the theater, and we all know a handful of show tunes and songs from their youth—"Good-bye, My Coney Island Baby," and "Never Say No" from *The Fantasticks* (Schmidt and Jones, 1960). Now, if we sing together, she'll gloat, "Our voices sound the same."

I recall a moment in the car at age four or five, enjoying that I knew the song she belted out in the front seat but singing quietly in the back. "Who's that singing?" she asked. I was silent. Another scene is from my crib: She sang "All the Pretty Little Horses," and I closed my eyes so she would think I was asleep. She turned to leave and I watched her in the dark, hoping she would stay and sing more but not making a sound. What was I avoiding? As I imagine the moment now, she turns to me and I can't breathe; I disappear. I feel no longing for her touch or embrace. My chest is tight and tears form. I want, but it's not safe.

My present-day compromise is to sing with her when we are at her house, after dinner, because it makes her very happy. I am supremely aware of how I hold my body, allowing my face to reflect the music and theatrical fun, but making only glancing eye contact with her. Even my sons have learned the tunes and sometimes join in. I'm aware that I use them as shields and worry that I haven't protected them well enough from their grandmother.

Saying this out loud hurts. I feel disloyal. Hearing it would tear her up. That's the dilemma.

As an aside, I remember a dream from before I was five: My father and I are driving along a highway. There is an elevated roadway to our right, and my mother speeds by on a motorcycle, driving the wrong way. I know she will crash, and then I hear a loud thump. Around seven or eight, I dreamed of her as a wizened old woman, coming at me through our back door; I am lying on my back on the kitchen floor and kick her away with powerful legs but fear she will return. In another dream, I come upon her and my father in our living room, tightly bound in white gauze like a spider's web, dead and faceless. More recently, and with more voice, I dream that she buzzes at me incessantly with ridiculous complaints. I yell at her to *shut up*—so satisfying!—but she is relentless.

Two: To protect myself from disappearing. My mother insists I am still her baby girl and wishes I'd sit on her lap; she walks around my house, asking, "Did I give you that?" about a vase or a painting; she is immediately anxious if I complain of some pain and offers six solutions to relieve her distress. My whole life, she would take my face in her hands, coming close, and tell me how much she loved me and how special I was. She saw herself, not me—unresponsive, enduring the moment. A few years ago, I told her I hated it when she did that—it felt intrusive, unboundaried. She looked at me, utterly uncomprehending. The next time we met, she moved to hug me but stepped back and said, "Oh, do you not want to be touched?" It was like there was something wrong with *me*.

Another example is my wedding. I pooh-poohed the need for a rehearsal, so when the moment came for my parents to walk me into the ceremony, we were winging it. My father took my hand, and my mother latched her arm around my waist. It was an agonizing moment. I thought perhaps it was a brief gesture and she'd let go, but she held tight, even as I twisted slightly and began to walk forward. I could not imagine stopping and asking her to release me or telling her it felt awful. What a scene that would be! It seemed I had no option but to proceed, working furiously inside to hold the experience as *mine* in spite of that familiar grip clawing me toward herself.

Three: To keep from wounding her. Here's the catch. She takes everything personally, imagines a perceived slight is planned to insult, rages when I make some claim for myself that doesn't suit her. When she's hurt, she lashes out with cutting words or ices me out with silence.

I don't remember Mother's Day being a big deal growing up. When I lived in New

The Road Goes Ever On and On

York City in my 20s, I probably sent a card or phoned her. One year shortly after I was married, I called to let her know we would be going to my husband's hometown to visit that weekend; I'd be back Sunday and would give her a call. There was a long silence. She repeated what I'd said to confirm and then added in a cold, angry voice, "Well, if you're not going to be here, don't bother calling me." I sputtered, my guts seizing up, my voice tightened with tears. It was like she'd punched me. We didn't speak for two months, and the following Mother's Day, I obediently arranged an outing, fuming.

A few years later, when both my boys were small, I began to feel angry about Mother's Day. I talked myself through multiple rationales about how it was *my* day, too, and how about if I wanted to spend it with my kids, doing whatever I wanted to do? I formulated a reasonable, well-argued presentation and called to suggest that we celebrate Mother's Day with her the Sunday before or after. That time we didn't speak for three months; finally, I suggested we go into family therapy.

The irony here is that—although over the course of several months I got to say much I wouldn't otherwise have spoken to her about our relationship—nothing really changed. She was uncomprehending in the therapist's office as I laid out my beefs. I looked beseechingly at him—surely he could see that this was her issue we were dealing with? Please just say she's wrong!—but got more family-systems framing and curiosity about where my father was in all this. Eventually, she and I no longer felt so angry and we stopped going. And Mother's Day is a duty day that I observe annually with little pleasure.

The Process of Unfolding

My internal rule about keeping silent has been slow to become visible. Its roots are deep in my family history: Ask about my parents fighting, burning a fur hat, throwing their wedding rings across a field? Nope. Express anger when I'm discouraged from applying to Harvard because it's so expensive but meantime they're renovating the house? Uh uhn. The directive to shut down my feelings, my wishes, my voice has been omnipresent.

In therapy and supervision, over 30-plus years, I've slowly and painfully come to see how the rule plays out in my adult life. I began to see how I didn't ask hard questions or make pointed observations with clients. I couldn't bring myself to let others know I needed referrals. I didn't fight with my co-therapist or insist we build up our group. In personal relationships—especially with women—I craved intimacy but was clumsy and guarded in reaching for it. Called out over and over (with love, I will say, and often by my therapist and supervisor) on underplaying my stronger, louder impulses, I finally began to distinguish between what felt like a *real* me and a well-entrenched role I'd been carrying on for decades.

Real me is a bit boisterous, often quite funny, loves to dance, can get mad and let you know about it, speaks up readily about wishes. I described in supervision group my experience of creating a false self as being like origami, where with each application of the silencing rule, I made another fold. The folds became intricate, one turning into the next, hiding previous folds and making new shapes. Unfolding was terrifying.

At AAP's 2014 I&C in St. Louis, I stood up in Community Meeting and talked about my mother troubles and how my parents and I were going to therapy. "Sometimes

I just wish she'd die already," I said, shaking, but not joking. More than one person responded later, suggesting I do a workshop on mothers. While I processed that idea over the winter, a friend recommended a book. Alison Bechdel's 2013 graphic memoir *Are You My Mother?* enraptured me. Bechdel's childhood with a theatrical mother and adult journeys through therapy felt wildly familiar. In the story, she works her way through Miller's *The Drama of the Gifted Child* (1997) and several volumes of Winnicott, parsing what she learns with us and her therapists. I was happy to get the précis of Winnicott's good-enough mother and the struggle of true self versus false self—the concept of the false self developing because the mother requires the infant to reflect *her* rather than display a true self. This not-good-enough-mother is the object the infant internalizes; as I parse it, this object is the self-silencing rule. To quote Bechdel:

> Here's the vital core of Winnicott's theory: The subject must destroy the object. And the object must survive this destruction. If the object doesn't survive, it will remain internal, a projection of the subject's self. If the object survives destruction, the subject can see it as separate (p. 267).

The following fall, I gave an I&C workshop titled "How to Kill Your Mother."

Origami Leaves Creases

The year my parents turned 76, I threw a big party and invited most of my friends (whom my parents adore and who, for the most part, find my mother much easier to tolerate than I do). At the time, my mother was living with a diagnosis of Hepatitis C (then considered treatable but incurable). My boys had recently been experimenting with origami, and I devised a plan to make one thousand cranes, a Japanese symbol of health and wellbeing. We spent two months folding, over and over, generating little birds. I threaded them by the hundreds in long strings, creating a display that consumed my living room. The night of the party, I made a little theater out of presenting her with a tiny scroll that related the legend of the thousand cranes and then led them to the big reveal.

It was a classic moment for me: doing something I think she'll like, wishing for that little space where my insides relax and I know I've got it right; I don't let myself hope further, reaching for contact with her, since that's more dangerous. She stepped into the living room and took in the flock, then turned to me in dismay and said, "But I'm not sick."

I was quiet.

The road goes ever on and on (as Tolkien tells us) (1954). My process of unfolding continues in fits and starts. Sometimes I find myself falling into the creases a fold has left behind; sometimes I rush forward and embrace a new design. When I am my true self, I feel amazing: powerful, whole, worthwhile. That is worth the journey. ▼

References:

Bechdel, A. (2013). *Are you my mother?: A comic drama.* Wilmington, DE: Mariner Books.

Jones, T. and Schmidt, H. (1968). *The fantasticks.* New York: Avon.

Miller, A. (1997). *The drama of the gifted child.* New York: Basic Books.

Tolkien, J.R.R. (1954). *The fellowship of the ring.* Sydney, Australia: Allen & Unwin.

Catherine B. Clemmer

CATHERINE B. CLEMMER, LCSW, has a private practice in Chapel Hill, North Carolina. She was an AAP Scholar in 2013 and joined in 2014. She led workshops at the 2016 and 2017 Summer Workshops and 2017 I&C that focused on experiencing connection without vision. These experiences allowed her to delve further into her own experiences being visually impaired. She is gaining awareness of ways she self-silences about her experiences and needs both with others and herself.
catherineclemmer@yahoo.com

I Got It

WHEN LAURA JUNE ASKED ME TO BE A PART OF THIS PANEL, I FELT SURPRISED. I don't think of myself as quiet and probably could benefit from silencing myself sometimes. Then I thought of my vision. I don't spend much time considering the vulnerabilities around my vision, much less how I silence myself about it. I have done a lot to convince others that my vision isn't a "thing."

I was diagnosed with Stargardt disease at age 14. Approximately 1 in 8-10,000 people have this disease. It is a recessive genetic eye disease that affects the retina and causes central vision loss. Additionally, it causes light sensitivity, difficulties transitioning from bright to dark spaces, and reduced color discrepancy. Over the years I developed strategies for accommodating myself to keep my vulnerability hidden.

I am now 41 and have had lots of practice at seeming as close to normal as possible. One trick I started using early was false eye contact. I direct my eyes so it appears to others I am looking them in the eye. However, my central vision is a large blind spot. I need to look off to the side to see someone's face, but I don't do that because it is strange and confusing for people. Another strategy is to reassure people I don't need help. I don't want to be seen as needy. So I present myself as being needless and able to do everything on my own. I go to great lengths to accommodate myself even if it means eye strain and extra time and energy. I pull out my phone to use the magnifier to read something instead of asking someone to read it for me. I walk up and down grocery store aisles multiple times trying to find an item instead of asking someone. When I do receive help, I validate that it is difficult to help me, thank them excessively, and apologize for needing help in the first place.

Having been diagnosed so young, I didn't want to speak up about my needs because I didn't want to be different. I tried my best to pass for sighted. My difference was exposed when I had to read something and needed to have it just a few inches from my face. In college, I worried that if I didn't handle things myself, there would not be anyone to help me and I would be completely lost. I was relieved that I achieved a D in my calculus class. I asked my professor if I could have a copy of her notes to keep at my desk since I couldn't see the board, but was told no. So I sat staring into space trying not to fall asleep. I felt proud when I made the UNC cheerleading team. I thought no one would know by watching me that I had a disability. I found out that some of the football players called me the "blind cheerleader." I worked to let that roll off my back. The most difficult moment was at practice one evening. The coach had us doing back tucks on the gymnastic floor. If we did it correctly, he pointed silently at us, which meant for us to move off the floor. Apparently he pointed at me, which of course I didn't see. He then told me to get my "Helen Keller ass off the floor." I held my head high and walked off the floor holding tightly in my mind to how his comment meant I'd done the back tuck correctly.

I worry about being experienced as a burden or incapable. Several years ago researchers isolated the gene that causes Stargardt. They are now doing clinical trials with gene replacement therapy. When I shared this with my husband at the time (now divorced), he said, "Does that mean I won't have to drive you everywhere anymore?" I recall a friend who kept her distance after my divorce. She later told me it was because she felt overwhelmed by my needs even though I never voiced them. I experienced discrimination at my first full-time job after college working as a research assistant. I self-disclosed during the interview about my vision. I later learned that I was kept from doing various tasks due to an assumption that I couldn't. I confronted my supervisor about my concerns and assured her I had tools that would allow me to perform needed duties. After that conversation and my self-accommodating, I was able to progress in my job. But after that experience, I never disclosed that I had a disability until I was hired.

After my divorce, I was thrust into single parenthood. I suddenly had to do everything alone both for myself and my children. As difficult as it was, I acknowledged I needed help. I reached out to Services for the Blind. I worked with an independent living specialist who led a cooking class and provided me with tools and gadgets to assist me with various home tasks. I was set up with a mobility and orientation specialist who provided me with a cane and lessons on how to use it.

When considering going to the Austin Institute & Conference in 2014, I was unable to find a travel buddy. I'd had my cane for a year but would not use it. If I wanted to travel alone, I would have to use it. I was faced with a choice: Use the cane, ask for help, and go to the conference, or stay in my hiding place safely tucked away at home. A friend dropped me off at the airport. I stepped out with my cane in hand and walked moving it from left to right. Someone came up to me and asked if I needed help. I found myself saying yes and feeling relieved to have the help. Once at the counter, I was asked if I needed assistance to my terminal. Again I said yes. Eventually a man approached with a wheelchair. My chest tightened and I felt as though everyone around me was staring. I explained I could walk just fine but could not see well enough to get to my terminal. The man left the wheelchair and held out his arm for me to hold on. He guided me to the front of the security lines. He then guided me to a chair at my terminal and

I Got It   **93**

informed the staff person at the desk that I would need assistance boarding the plane. I was still uncomfortable with the feeling that everyone's eyes were on me. Soon I heard an announcement over the speaker saying anyone needing special assistance could now board. I stood up, not sure exactly where I was supposed to go. Someone came up and asked if I needed assistance boarding. I said yes and was guided down the hall and to the opening of the plane. I was greeted with friendly hellos as a flight attendant checked my ticket and led me to my seat. The conference, too, was a different experience from those previous. So many of you approached me with words of encouragement and offers of assistance. I haven't put my cane down since.

This is the hardest part for me to share. Now I have to tell you how I feel about being visually impaired. Underneath the humor, fierce independence, and false eye contact, I often feel distant and lonely. I wish I could look at my children's faces and see the specific details of a dimple or a freckle. I wish I could go to dinner with my boyfriend and actually see the look in his eyes when he sees me, or a smile on his face when I make him laugh. I want to see when my clients have tears just starting to glisten in their eyes or the beginnings of a smile.

I sat in my therapist's office discussing this talk. I felt frustrated that I couldn't get at why I feel cut off emotionally from my vision. He often sees how things are harder for me that I don't notice. Sometimes I'm talking, and he will say, "And then there's the added difficulty of the vision." It feels novel to me when he mentions it. In this session, I finally heard myself say, "I don't want anyone to know about the loneliness of blindness," and felt tears burning my eyes. We sat silently for a moment. This was a silence that honored what was spoken for the first time.

I led my first process group at the 2016 Summer Workshop. I had everyone wear sleep masks to explore connecting through other senses. I experienced something I did not anticipate: For the first time since I was 14, I was the most-sighted person in the room. I felt connected to the others and enjoyed being the guide. For the last third of the group, I had everyone take their masks off and reorient to having their sight. The remaining part of the group was to be spent with masks off to compare connecting through other senses with connecting visually.

I was caught off guard by the rush of sadness that came over me. It felt like everyone reentered the sighted world and left me behind. I was back in my familiar place of being a sense down and less connected than everyone else. I immediately felt my confidence slip. I worried that, since I could not see, I would be ineffective as the leader for the remainder of the group. I got quiet, trusting the group would be able to process without me. I worked hard to shove away my sadness and feelings of abandonment. Someone asked me how I was doing. At first, I laughed nervously, feeling exposed. I couldn't see anyone's faces to get feedback about how I was being received. I spoke a little about how I was not expecting to have an emotional reaction to the shift without the masks on, but it was fine because the group wasn't about me. I swallowed hard and fought back tears. The group lovingly encouraged me to speak more about my experience and said, just because I was the leader didn't mean I couldn't get something out of the group. I spoke a little more about feeling left and a loss of confidence and competence. The tears came. I felt ashamed and embarrassed. All of my messages of being weak and needy were rushing through my mind. My heart swelled with gratitude and love when the group decided to put their masks back on to reconnect with me. I have done the group twice more, and each time am filled with a similar sadness.

Writing this, I feel lonely in the separateness of my blind world from your sighted world. My fear is you pity me, see me as weak, see me as dependent or needy, or see me as incapable. I assume you want to hear a story about resilience and strength, about how I never let my visual impairment weigh me down, and how I will conquer the world and let nothing stop me. That is part of me too. There's also the silent and previously hidden part that is lonely and scared. She lives alone in the visually impaired world separate from all of you in the sighted world. In embracing my authentic voice, I am using words to introduce her to you.

The world responds to me differently when I allow my needs to show. Bus drivers in my town know me and look out for me. People working in stores come up and ask if I need help. Sometimes people standing beside me at crosswalks will tell me when the light is green and I can walk. Strangers I pass walking say hi—I am guessing previously they would only smile. Cars stop to let me cross the street. I keep my day-to-day world small so that I can navigate it alone, but I feel taken care of by my small community. It's not all sunshine and roses. I also notice that sometimes on the bus people choose to stand when the only vacant seat is beside me. Sometimes the tone of voice people use with me is slower and slightly louder, as if they are speaking to a child or an elderly person. I get stares from people. Overall it feels freeing to embrace my disability and allow my authentic voice to be heard. I still have work to do around asking for and accepting help instead of immediately saying, "I got it," but I feel good about allowing more of me to be seen and dropping the façade of being needless. ▼

Sometimes being a friend means mastering the art of timing. There is a time for silence. A time to let go and allow people to hurl themselves into their own destiny. And a time to prepare to pick up the pieces when it's all over.

—Octavia Butler

Scott Baum

SCOTT BAUM, PhD, ABPP, is a clinical psychologist and bioenergetic therapist living and practicing in NYC.
docsbpsych@aol.com

Unspeakable

Unspeakable in that it may not be spoken—and of such pain and terribleness that it cannot be rendered and expressed in words.

THIS HAS TURNED OUT TO BE THE MOST DIFFICULT ARTICLE I HAVE WRITTEN FOR *VOICES*. I have already accidentally deleted a draft. Why is that? Certainly, what I have to say, and have said in other articles, is difficult to hear. The plight of those of us severely abused, terrified, annihilated psychically and emotionally, used, transformed to malevolence—all things I have written about—are difficult to say and to hear. And, indeed, nearly impossible to work with in psychotherapy unless one can hear the language not only of the unspoken, but of what cannot, and may not, be spoken. It cannot be spoken because the capacity to join language with experience to convey meaning has been destroyed. It cannot be spoken because traumatizing assault on all levels of being has stopped development of complex, felt, emotional and psychic capacities. It cannot be spoken because the politics of the field of psychotherapy, of therapists, hews closely enough to the politics of current human societies that the suppressive effects of denial, ignorance, fear, and a refusal to face what we human beings can do to each other begin to interfere with successful psychotherapy.

Perhaps I can relieve my anxiety about writing this, a bit, by making a plea for indulgence. I'm angry and I'm afraid. I have a life-long identification with my father, an angry, defiant man who was both thoroughly corrupted by self-interest and courageously and rightly outspoken about social ills. And I have an identity as a person who speaks vehemently, or when more grounded, passionately. My motives for doing so are inevitably mixed with virulent strains of malevolent grandiosity and domineering superiority. So, take the force of what I say with a bit of preparation to deflect, if necessary, to broaden, even to leaven. But, I am trying to embody the theme, to work on the edge of my unspoken, or unspeakable—as I have done in my personal psychotherapy sessions for close now to nearly half a century.

I am old enough in the field to have seen the philosophy of psychotherapy move through significant stages, starting with the pessimism of psychoanalytic thinking. It's not hard for me to understand that surrender to despair about human beings when so much of psychoanalytic theory was formulated by people who saw the emergence of the worst of human malevolence on a world-wide scale. Many of them were directly targeted by it. Then I saw psychotherapy embrace the openness and promise of the "Summer of Love." In fact, some of the impetus for that flow to goodness and pleasure came from movements in psychotherapy. I've seen the competing models of psyche/no psyche, the broadening focus from the individual in distress to the system both in distress and causing distress, even a brief experiment in community intervention. The challenge of retaining hope and belief in people that they will choose goodness is always with us, but right now that hope is challenged again in a more frightening way than it has been in a while.

I have seen a deepening acknowledgment by theorists and therapists of the damage wrought on patients organized as borderline and schizophrenic, and the way that damage manifests itself in the inner reality in which people organized that way live our lives. And I have seen the difficulty that therapists have, those who do not live in that universe of people so organized, and perhaps some who do, in apprehending that experience. I am not talking about people who believe the conditions are caused by some unicorn of a brain problem. Whether there is anything to that is, frankly, irrelevant. There is more than enough, too much, psychological, emotional, and somatopsychic harm caused by the way people treat each other to occupy the central focus of our researches.

Why not focus on that? If not in the society at large, in our field? Here's a little clinical example. I am newly a grandfather, my first grandchild. I cannot tell people, including friends who are also colleagues, that this child does not evoke in me the doting thrill of grandparenthood they all believe in, and many have experienced first-hand. I won't go into how I was emptied out as an infant and child and adolescent and young adult (traumatic treatment does not end in childhood, most of the time). I have written about that elsewhere. Or how I was transformed to malevolence. Wrote about that also. Rather, I want to focus on the question of why people cannot believe, cannot tolerate this reality.

I will say that one reason it is difficult for me has to do with the fact that this child is also the grandchild of my first, late wife, who was a member of this Academy, and who, in lending me a soul, and fighting with me to behave as if I had one, may have made possible this experience I am having. Even with the very good psychotherapists with whom I have worked, I don't know if the life I am living, good in so many ways, for which I am immensely grateful, could be without her. I am now in a second marriage, also to a therapist, who can also bear the unbearable, face the emptiness I experience, encounter the malevolence, and remain attached and connected to me in ways that enable me to do the same. In the metric of modern discourse in psychotherapy, I am very resilient; I have done a lot with what I have. But this focus misses, or deflects, or ignores, or denies, or fends off, the unspoken.

So, why not focus on what we therapists have learned from exposure to the unspeakable and unspoken realities our borderline and schizophrenic patients present to us? You may think this is an exaggerated point. But, here is a small example. When I submitted a workshop proposal for AAP's Institute & Conference on this theme, it was accepted, and I am grateful. The planning committee asked that I permit a change in the workshop copy because I included in my proposal a focus on work specifically with people organized as borderline or schizophrenic. The committee felt that would narrow the appeal of the presentation because they believe that relatively few Academy members work with people organized that way. I have no trouble acceding to their request; they want my program to succeed, and so do I. I have no doubt that they have the best intentions for the conference and the participants at heart. But, I am startled. In the clinical world I live in, people's psychotherapy practices can be filled with people organized in these ways unless therapists are very careful to balance their case load, or to screen out such people, which is difficult to do since many of us have perfectly adaptive appearances and don't know ourselves what we are dealing with until well into the therapy. (When I received the program for the conference I saw that the description I provided for my workshop was, in fact, not changed. I am touched and heartened by the committee's decision.)

Therapists are, by and large, optimistic people, believing in the possibility of change toward pleasure and goodness and freedom not only in the individuals they work with, but in people in general. That belief and conviction may emerge from the therapist's life experience. It may be a philosophical position. It can, as all beliefs and convictions can, distort or skew or bias a person to see things a certain way. Sometimes people are hearteningly courageous enough to face their biases, even prejudices, and reconsider important positions they hold. I presented a keynote address last year at a bioenergetic conference. My presentation was paired with one by Alan Kalpin, a lovely, warm psychiatrist from Canada. At the end he told me that what I presented opened a new vista for him. He would consider my experience that anhedonia in borderline and schizophrenic people, like in me, could represent an inability to experience benevolence. And that that being true significantly affected the thrust and understanding of psychotherapeutic treatment with people so organized. I could not have asked for a more receptive, respectful response.

To be maximally receptive to the unspoken and the unspeakable—both because of the enormity of what has been done, and because speaking of it is prohibited—requires an openness to being exposed to realities most therapists would like to believe occur to people other than those who can appear in our consultation rooms. The saying about sticks and stones is incorrect. Words, gestures, tones, looks and the destructive energies that accompany them when applied to a vulnerable person over a long enough time can do as much, or sometimes more, damage than physical violence, although the two are actually rarely far from each other. What limits our consciousness of these realities? What makes it funny when a keynote speaker at an AAP conference refers to his "psychotic" moment in a way intended to elicit a laugh, and it does? There is nothing funny about the experience of psychosis.

I have, my whole life, avoided stimulation that would overwhelm my defenses. I strive to enter the edges of decompensation, to remain barely organized in the disorganization, so that I can re-enter and re-inhabit parts of my being. The experience of despair, of black-hole emptiness is awful. My mother's immersion in that saturated me. Whatever vitality I have is limited by the preponderance of my energy being devoted to holding myself together. I understand that I might not look like this is happening. But I am perplexed when psychotherapists have difficulty believing it is happening when I tell them about it.

In this time in our history, in the world's history, knowing how interpersonal treatment murders souls, stunts emotional and psychic development, interferes with understanding, and precludes choices of life and love seems critical. We therapists know things about what is happening to harm people immersed in hatred and in polarization, in superiority and self-serving; we know both the intrapsychic terrain and some of its effects on the interpersonal and social worlds. Few are listening to us. That is unfortunate. Are we listening to each other, to our patients? Does hearing the unspoken and the unspeakable call us at least to talk with each other?

It may be that speaking what cannot be spoken will make no difference—although psychodynamic psychotherapy is predicated on the principle that it does. My experience says it does. Here is what my therapist, Mike Eigen, said about me:

> Here is a little example. It is about a man I wrote about in Toxic Nourishment and Damaged Bonds. I called him Milton. He is a man who has been in pain all his life, pain that won't go away. I don't know whether it will ever go away or not. I have no idea and he doesn't either. It is awful. He would commit suicide if not for what I'm not sure—maybe his children, maybe something more, a kind of deep dedication to the truth of life, his truth. He is devoted to inner truthfulness. We have been together many years, and he was in therapy many more years with people before me. He is trying to make contact—with himself, with life. He is committed to his search. To be present in his search yet not able to be present in life—to be present at all is a plus. For some being present to one's non-presence may be better than not being there and not knowing it. For Milton, it's a must.
>
> A few weeks ago he said, "I feel my father killed me or some part of me." And I said I absolutely believe you. And he weeps. After a long silence he says, "When I heard your words I felt an entity leave me." That's the little vignette. He's not cured, I'm not cured. I'm in pain, he's in pain. I'm broken, he's broken. But at this moment, this one little moment when he felt, actually felt, took many years to find. These weren't wasted years. They could look wasted. Some therapists wouldn't have been able to stand it. But these years weren't wasted because a moment arrived when he felt my belief in his pain. For an instant he believed that I actually believed he was in pain and that his pain could be permanent. He heard me and for a moment felt my affirmation of the truth of his feeling. A feeling that came through was "Yes I absolutely, absolutely believe you." And he said "When I heard you, when I heard your words I felt an entity leave me." Now I know that if one entity leaves there are probably a million more. But it was a precious moment that took years to happen. No insurance company would pay for this moment. But it is an eternal moment. A moment that makes a difference to the universe forever. And some of you may be feeling ripples of it today (Eigen, 2010, pp. 18-19).

At this moment in time when so many cry out to be heard, even in what cannot be spoken, when so many are crying, we have the knowledge and the skill to hear, to feel, to apprehend that which cannot be spoken. We don't know what the effect of hearing will be. We know what the effect of not hearing has been. We'll need each other's support to do it. ▼

References
Eigen, M. (2010). *Madness and murder.* London: Karnac Press.

Kristie Nies & Mike Geringer

KRISTIE NIES, PHD, is the lead neuropsychologist at OhioHealth, where she engages in clinical and administrative activities. She is fiercely committed to friends and family, Ashtanga yoga, and transformational work.
krisnies@gmail.com

J. MICHAEL "MIKE" GERINGER, PHD, is O'Bleness professor of international strategy and director of research at Ohio University's College of Business. In addition to professional and academic leadership activities, he has received numerous awards, including the Decade Award for research impact, Lifetime Achievement Award, and University Distinguished Teacher Award. A consultant and visiting professor on six continents, he was executive producer for an Emmy-award recipient's CD.
Geringer@ohio.edu

The Business of Silence:
Communication Without Words

> Silence is the only language spacious enough to include everything and to keep us from slipping back into dualistic judgments and divisive words.
> —Richard Rohr

> Silence remains, inescapably, a form of speech.
> —Susan Sontag

COMMUNICATION CAN BE A CHALLENGE UNDER THE BEST OF CONDITIONS. While the meaning of words can be problematic at times, silence may be even more prone to misinterpretation and associated complications. We are a couple navigating recent love in later life. Effective communication, including silence, is critically important to avoid shipwreck during the inevitable rough seas that such a journey will entail. Disclaimer: We met on the online dating site Match.com which, as a platform, lends itself to long periods of silence, at least during the initial contact and courting phase of a relationship. In our case, the time between meeting online and meeting in person was relatively brief. As we continue to grow as a couple, we are learning to hold the tension between both sound and silence and—since we do not live in the same city—between proximity and separation. We are introverts and both value cerebral process, each of which entails some degree of silence. However, we view the world through very different lenses. Kristie is a neuropsychologist, yogi, and recovering psychotherapist; Mike is a university research professor, executive trainer, and peripatetic consultant in international business strategy. This article describes our efforts to span these professional and cultural differences and to understand the different languages that comprise the spoken and unspoken word in couples work. Perhaps silence could be considered a universal language.

Like the old *Rocky and Bullwinkle* cartoon that had two titles per episode (e.g., "The Road to Ruin or Mine Over Matter"), the alternative title for this piece was "Silence in Self-Help Couples Work: Sacred Space or Weapon of Mass Destruction?" This dichotomy prompted an analysis of advantages and disadvantages of silence as a form of communication, which ultimately led to the delineation of five different kinds of silence:

1. Logistical silence
2. Silence of solitude
3. Silence of evasion
4. Respectful silence
5. A touch of silence

We will describe our experience of each kind of silence, potential benefits and inherent problems associated with each type, and one or more possible solutions.

As a precursor to our discussion, let's put silence into context regarding the authors' upbringing. In Kristie's family of origin, repression was the name of the game. Silence, and its close cousin absence, was often interrupted by violence. She learned that silence was combustible. To her, absence can feel like abandonment. Silence, on a primitive level, can feel life threatening. Mike's early experience with his family included extensive conversation (e.g., discussion of events, activities, family news), but feelings were implicitly taboo as a topic appropriate for discourse, resulting in an environment that was confusing and frustrating. There was connection of a sort, but it felt incomplete and unsatisfying, and escape to outdoor activities and books brought the deeper connection he sought. The price he paid for these excursions to solitude was feeling isolated and different, estranged from his feelings and disoriented navigating the cocktail party of life. These very different experiences of silence have the potential to create discord in our relationship.

Logistical Silence

> The scary thing about distance is you don't know whether they'll miss you or forget you.
> —Nicholas Sparks, *The Notebook*

> Though silence is not necessarily an admission, it is not a denial, either.
> —Cicero

We both enjoy our respective professional work and our frequent contact with each other throughout the day, but workplace commitments and relationship maintenance can be at cross purposes. That is, there can be long stretches in the day during which we cannot communicate synchronously with the other. In addition, Mike's work typically has him traveling internationally about once a month for anywhere from 5 days to 3 weeks, resulting in extended periods of time when he is on a plane, in a different time zone, or in countries with limited Internet or phone infrastructure.

An inherent problem with logistical silence is the potential for distortion and disconnection. Whether the imposed silence is due to normal domestic workday commitments or those associated with travel, these periods of silence can make it challenging to feel connected, to be attuned to what each is experiencing and feeling during a day, and to address the small and sometimes not-so-small life and relationship issues that arise. While email and texting can be useful in these situations, these modes of communication embody obvious limitations that can serve as a source of confusion and/or distress, depending on each partner's historical emotional experience with silence. For example, Mike's communication style often includes brief "directives" such as, "You can get concert tickets." In the absence of context, this communication style is particularly triggering for Kristie, who hears it as a command. Her first reaction is something along the lines of, "You're not the boss of me." This perceived edict guarantees that no tickets will be purchased.

One possible solution to logistical silence is to cultivate a benefit-of-the-doubt attitude. To do this well, it is important for each person to know their triggers. Armed with this self-knowledge, it may be easier to accept the emotional reactivity as, perhaps, coming from within one's own head rather than from a partner's ill intent. Physical separation and communication silence need not imply emotional withdrawal or similar interpretations. In the long run, we need to address our communication style regarding frequency, mode, and message. In the short run, employing the "note to self" approach, Kristie can say, "I know what he means," while also conveying the desire for requests rather than demands.

Silence of Solitude

> If I cannot understand my friend's silence, I will never get to understand his words.
> —Enoch Powell

> Pratyahara is the movement of the mind towards silence rather than towards things.
> —Donna Farhi

We are both accustomed to a great deal of solitude. Even in the absence of physical or work-related factors, we both employ various methods of "aloneness" to self-regulate (e.g., yoga, meditation, nature walks, cycling). Whether it is a thorny work-related conundrum or some aspect of the relationship creating strife, there can be periods of silence as each person comes to terms with the issue or situation. In this respect, these periods can provide healthy space to think, to sharpen one's focus, to consider emotions and context, to revitalize, and to connect with ourselves to achieve balance and be fully present in the relationship.

An inherent problem with this type of silence is that if the intent is not clearly communicated, the behavior can be seen by the other person as controlling, distancing, withholding, alienating, withdrawing, etc. Probing or pushing for premature emergence from solitude can result in conflict. If one person's demands exceed the other's capabilities, retaliatory silence can ensue, potentially unleashing a vicious circle of stimulus and response patterns that can take on a ruinous life of its own. Also, non-sharing can result in a monologue conducted within ourselves, with potential for misattribution, stagnation of communication, and creation or expansion of factors that may ultimately diminish or eliminate the potential for successful resolution of underlying problems.

One possible solution to the silence of solitude is to be proactive. Communicating and letting your partner know you will be unavailable for a period of time may prevent misunderstanding and misinterpretation of the associated period of silence. While biorhythms may have fallen out of favor, there is something to be said for being mindful of the contraction/expansion of various aspects of ourselves and our partners. Energy for the relationship may shift and fluctuate and be a positive indicator of the need for separateness in the togetherness.

Silence of Evasion

> Once a word has been allowed to escape, it cannot be recalled.
>
> —Horace

> You can't put the shit back in the donkey.
>
> —Tony Soprano

Conversation that deftly circumvents a "hot" topic could be considered silence of evasion. Avoiding an issue allows interaction to continue and possibly mitigates the reactions that complete silence might provoke. Such delay may also allow the partner who is avoiding a topic time to think through the issue, promoting comfort, confidence, and balance.

An inherent problem with evasion is the potential to let silence substitute for talking about feelings, concerns, fears, conflict, and misunderstandings, while feeding the fantasy that our partner can read our minds. We don't address the initial problem and are disappointed that our partner is not a perfect mirror.

A recent rupture highlights the potentially destructive nature of evasion, even if (or maybe especially if) it is not conscious. For us, Sunday nights are fraught, as they herald physical separation for the upcoming work week. In this instance, we had just returned from a weekend visiting family. The trip involved a long drive and, well...family. We had just moved into a new house together, still without most of the furniture and other comforts of a home. Mike was about to leave on a long business trip. In the stress of it all, we miscommunicated and missed connecting fully before parting company. We chose instead to shadow box in our own heads, which fueled disappointment and hurt. In hindsight, a conversation about the enormity of the move, Mike's potential role in Kristie's family, and the depth of the longing and dependency that got activated by his impending absence would have served us well.

One solution is to be vigilant about not using evasion as a means of conflict resolution (i.e., keeping the peace). Timing and delivery are also important considerations when raising an issue. Checking in to assure that the time is optimal for an important discussion without frightening the other person is a skill worth cultivating. Also, couples may do well to use the HALT acronym employed by Alcoholics Anonymous. Do not undertake controversial communication when either person is Hungry, Angry, Lonely, or Tired.

Respectful Silence

> The biggest communication problem is we do not listen to understand. We listen to reply.
> —Stephen R. Covey

> We have two ears and one mouth so that we can listen twice as much as we speak.
> —Epictetus

Silence is essential for effective—and especially reflective—listening. In this regard, periods of silence in conversation can be a sign of respect. Taking time to consider a statement or a question before responding can convey respect and gravitas, assuming the response is truly reflective and not a scene-stealing attempt to talk about oneself. Equally destructive is impulsively blurting out an ill-considered response to fill the void in a discussion. Silence, followed by an attuned response, can promote order and calmness during a conversation. It can convey a sense of being seen and heard that reinforces the notion that companionable quiet can foster a healthy relationship.

An inherent problem with this type of silence springs from fear. The speaker may fear he or she is babbling or taking up too much time. Alternatively, the speaker may fear that the other person is not getting it, disagrees but is withholding that opinion, or is bored or zoned out.

One solution is to punctuate pockets of silence with comforting nonverbal communication (e.g., nodding the head or other acknowledgment that one is still present in the conversation, albeit silently). Attuned, accurate, reflective listening can calm the soul of the speaker. Nonjudgmental silence, reflecting that one is indeed *listening* to the other and striving for full understanding without interruption, can promote comprehensive explanation and sharing of key ideas or concerns, particularly those of a more complex nature. Recognizing a partner's desire or need for silence as an active aspect of listening and attentiveness, and accepting this state, can help build trust and promote sharing and deeper exploration of problems and feelings.

A Touch of Silence

Touch has a memory.

—John Keats

Touch is far more essential than our other senses. ... It's ten times stronger than verbal or emotional contact.

—Saul Schanberg

The physical bond that many couples share cannot readily be translated into words. Touching, hand holding, hugging, slow dancing, massaging, kissing, and more explicitly sexual activity (which may or may not be silent) all convey a message. This type of silence feels like the most complicated one and, therefore, the most difficult to flesh out, so to speak. Love is generally a full contact sport. The ability of each partner to manage one's needs and desires while being mindful of the other person's wellbeing is a couple skill worth honing. What transpires physically between two people can reflect mere habit, a need, pleasure for pleasure's sake, or an intentional way to reinforce the depth of connection.

Several problems come to mind with this type of silence. Each person may have a different comfort level with physicality and/or sexuality. The intended message and the perceived message associated with touch may also differ, perhaps dramatically, which can create or exacerbate an issue. Pushing a physical agenda before establishing requisite trust, or before the partner has allowed these communication channels to open, can be unsatisfying for either or both people. Another potential problem is the possibility of sexualizing emotion or using touch to avoid a needed discussion.

How to address these problems? Identifying the intent behind physical contact is paramount to ensuring healthy interaction. For example, seeking the reassurance of a warm hug as a way to manage a negative emotion such as anger is likely to be a short-term fix that can create a long-term problem. Similarly, pleasing a partner sexually as a way to make up for some perceived or real infraction may not be the best solution. Then again, it might be, as long as the intent is communicated clearly and both people are in agreement. The body keeps the score and a physical action that only reflects misattunement may result in a zero-sum game, or worse.

Summary

> In human intercourse, the tragedy begins not when there is misunderstanding about words, but when silence is not understood.
>
> —Henry David Thoreau

> Silence is also conversation.
>
> —Ramana Maharshi

Moments of silence are unavoidable in relationships, and these moments can be healthy and invigorating or damaging and draining. Silence is worth second-guessing as it has many potential origins and meanings. If silence feels confrontational, you may view it as an opportunity to check in with your partner and confirm or disconfirm an initial impression. Rather than assuming silence is based on negative, indifferent, or disruptive factors, consider instead an alternative interpretation (e.g., reflection of peacefulness, contentment, or respect).

Even in the face of silence, there are times to "use your words" and to do so constructively and effectively. Efforts to clarify silence and its meaning, to indicate whether one needs space or not, is energy well spent. Honoring the need for space and embracing the positive aspects of silence can provide a strong foundation for mutual respect and for confidence and security in the communication at hand and in the relationship as a whole. Finding a safe and affirming space within the realm of silence, finding peace and trust within the absence of words, can be the foundation for a self-renewing and sustainable relationship.

Silence can include implicit rules, assumptions, hopes, fears, looks, touch, and all that is unconscious. Ultimately, depending on how well we conceive and implement it within a relationship, quietude can enhance and/or diminish intimate communication. The process of writing this article together has increased our respective tolerance of, and respect for, silence. The process also raised some issues (e.g., competition, vulnerability) that required thoughtful silent consideration as well as vigorous debate. Our understanding of the ways we use silence, constructively and destructively, has expanded as a result of this undertaking.

The theme throughout this article is self-awareness and communication. We have committed to actively practicing good couple-care, as well as good self-care, to prevent the equivalent of a silent relationship heart attack. As one way to honor this lifelong process, and as a tip of the hat to Match.com, we have decided to rewrite our profiles each year on our anniversary and to share these revisions exclusively with each other. This will be one way of communicating and confirming that our match remains strong. ▼

My Patients Think I'm Crazy

Maury Joseph

My patients think I'm crazy.

A woman was pleading,
"I don't know what to do with my husband!"
I smiled, "How wonderful!"
Up til then she had always known exactly what to do
And always lost herself in the doing.

My patients think I'm crazy.

A man spoke, under great pressure,
"Doctor, I'm confused!"
I offered, "Congratulations!
This is one of the things that can happen
When we begin to think for ourselves."

My patients think I'm crazy.

"I am so nervous about relapsing!" another one said.
"Good," I said,
and felt it inside,
so happy that she finally feared what had long hurt her.

My patients think I'm crazy.

One said, "Dr! I feel like I'm losing my edge at work."
I praised her.
You see, her edge had been a fantasy
And she had nearly died trying to realize it.

My patients think I'm crazy.

One told me, "Doctor, I'm having nightmares"
"Thank god," I said to myself,
"She's finally dreaming."

My patients think I'm crazy.

A man said he was awoken at 3am
By his own voice screaming for help.
Joyous tears came to my eyes.
For the first time I was not alone
in hearing the call.

My patients think I'm crazy.

Closings
Part 2

Ellen Weber Libby

ELLEN WEBER LIBBY, PHD, says, "The process of deciding when to close a practice is more layered, more detailed, and much richer than an article of 2,000 words can reflect. I invite people to interact with me around this exhilarating unfolding of personal growth generated by thoughts of retirement. Please share with me your experiences."
ewlibby@gmail.com

Editor's note: The first part of Ellen's article, about her process deciding to retire, ran in the Winter 2017 issue.

CHOOSING TO RETIRE WAS A COMPLICATED PROCESS AND DIFFICULT DECISION. But it paled in comparison to my anxiety as I anticipated telling my patients. These intense, long-term relationships, many 30 years and older, celebrated the profoundness of my rich career. My decision to retire reflected acceptance of my aging, not fatigue with the work.

When I contemplated locking my office door for the last time, I knew the psychotherapy stirred by my retirement would impact my patients' abilities to move on. How much time to allow for the issues generated by my leaving? Ultimately, 5 to 6 months emerged as the window with which I was most comfortable.

Too little notice would limit the potential of the evolving work. What my announcement set in motion would stir complicated feelings. Further, in groups that I singly led, my retirement would force an ending of the group and, most likely, the members' relationships with each other. With too much notice, the work might be derailed by patient beliefs that, "We have plenty of time for our good-bye. For now, I want to talk about...."

In making my announcement, I would be interjecting my issues on the therapy, a behavior I studiously avoided over the years. I knew the content of my leaving would leave me vulnerable to patient projections rooted in losses, separations and abandonments. I was anxious and frightened, feeling more vulnerable then I ever had. In many moments I asked myself, "What the hell are you doing, leaving work you love so much?"

I obsessed over the words of my announcement, a cover for my unease.

I could not anticipate my reactions when telling patients: Would I be emotional? Would that be ok? Would I sound too tight and uncomfortable? Would I get pulled into saying too much? Would I cut off my patients' process? I needed to begin the process of announcing my plans to retire. I needed a trial run.

I began by telling two patients, neither of whom I saw in groups. One, an elderly gentleman, represented those patients who typically stroked my narcissism. As a therapist, I could count on patients like him to make me feel competent, successful and important. The second person, a bipolar, borderline woman in her 40s, never fought directly with me, but rather, acted out her hostilities. She, and patients like her, could leave me feeling defeated, frustrated, and incompetent.

Morgan was homebound and widowed. Among his many health issues was a hearing loss; after six years of working with audiologists, he still had not found a satisfactory hearing aid. We often explored a possible connection between this experience and his preference for not wanting to hear anything that would stir his anger or unhappiness.

E: Morgan, I want you to know that I am retiring June 30.

M: What? You have to leave early today?

E: No, I am not leaving early today. I am retiring June 30.

M: What? So what time are you leaving today?

E: Morgan, I am not leaving early today. I will be here for the full time. What I said was I am retiring at the end of June.

M: Oh! (Slight pause. Nervous cough. Longer pause.) I am happy for you. (Pause.) So, when do you think we should wrap up between now and then? I know what you consider important: my needing more social contact.

E: We'll have time to figure all that out.

M: (Pause; sadness overcomes his face.)

E: You seem thoughtful.

Morgan then proceeded to talk about his unfinished business with his wife, Mary, who had died three years earlier. Morgan ended the session with uncharacteristic tears saying, "I want to do better in my good-bye to you than I did with her."

A good beginning. I hadn't crumbled knowing how lonely and emotionally isolated Morgan would be without me and felt more confident to tackle the work ahead.

Jeri, the second patient I told, functioned in a demanding job, but her personality adversely impacted most of her relationships. Her response was as anticipated:

J: If you knew you were going to retire in June, I don't get why you insisted on billing me for my missed appointment last month. But then again, you seldom see my side of it. I always play by the rules. When I ask you for an exception, you never go along. That's so unfair.

E: I am wondering if you are asking me to make an exception and continue to see you after June.

J: You always turn it in to the relationship. It isn't always about you. No, I don't care if you retire. If I did, it wouldn't matter anyway. You do what you want. I just think it unfair that you billed me for my missed appointment. If you are retiring, you don't need the money. I don't know why I even brought it up.

E: Maybe in this moment it is important to talk about how I disappoint you and let you down.

J: There you go again. No, you don't disappoint me. You do what you want. It isn't just about money. A few weeks ago, I wanted to cut back to every other week and you said no, knowing you were going to retire soon. Oh! That makes me so mad. So unfair. It isn't ok to do what I want, which is to have some money to spend on other things, but it is ok to do what you want, like bill me.

The session knocked against this patient's core belief that her needs are not acknowledged. The experience reminded me that regardless of how well I presented my goodbye, patients would respond in the context of their characters.

I survived the guilt and sadness evoked by Morgan. I survived the feelings of relief and regret that I hadn't been more effective in helping Jeri. I felt prepared for the next step: going public with my announcement.

My Announcement

The first group I told was one in which I had a co-therapist. If the group pulled me into saying more than I wanted, I trusted my co-therapist to gently pull me back. Some people had been participants in this high-functioning group for most of its duration, about 30 years. I knew it would be hard for me to leave the group, the patients, and my co-leader. And, I knew it would be equally hard for them to lose me.

With my announcement, profound sadness permeated the group. I had witnessed the growth of these eight people over many years, but I would not "be around to celebrate" future births, marriages, career successes or graduations. Tears, group members' and mine, filled the room. Their grief was palpable that this co-leadership would end. In the moment, I questioned my decision to retire: Was I making a mistake?

Another group consisted of people about my age. One member, recently retired, felt joined with me in the journey of exploring retirement. Some group members aligned with her. However, others aligned with a woman who expressed feelings of abandonment, outraged that I would retire before her journey was complete. This tension reflected the process common to this group, the push and pull of going deeper in the work versus appreciating what one had. The honesty of the struggle and the group's willingness to stay with its process moved me, again raising the question of why I was retiring.

The response of a couples group was indifference. Their primary concern was losing the other group members. These men and women had learned to rely on other group members as intermediaries in their marital conflicts and feared that without another to intervene, their spouses would be burdened with hurtful projections.

In individual work, the rawness not expressed in groups surprised me. One patient walked into my office, looked at me, and before saying a word ran to the bathroom to throw up. Another likened saying good-bye to me to the pain of a parent helplessly witnessing a child die: Children are not supposed to die first, and therapists are not supposed to leave first. Other patients felt envy, far stronger than any expressed in group, in witnessing me move on with my life.

The Psychotherapy of Saying Good-bye

Clients begin psychotherapy stirred by events, behaviors, and symptoms unique to them. But common to most therapies are underlying struggles of attaching and separating. Now, in the therapy framed by my good-bye, I expected unfinished issues of

Closings: Part 2   **109**

attachment and separation to be stirred, the expression of each imprinted by the given patient's unique history.

Most patients were stirred to reexamine old, painful ruptures. Fury was expressed at mothers for not having intervened when fathers had abused them. Other patients tapped into rage at spouses who had deceived them. Long-repressed emotions bubbled for abortions that had occurred many years earlier. Some patients discovered the pain of repressed abandonments by trusted clergy who had been sexually exploitive or a former therapist who had died suddenly, pain that had not previously surfaced in the therapy. Each patient's history informed the work we would co-create in the last months of being together.

The work of the ensuing 5 months was profound. It was guided, first, by my belief that our good-bye should not be compressed into our final sessions. While accepting that no good-bye would be complete, I believed that using all the time available to us would help bridge the gap between therapy with me and life after.

My second belief, the need for patients to self-affirm, challenged my importance to them. While a strong and trusting attachment with the therapist is essential for patient growth, it can easily be confused with successful therapy. When it is, patient's separation anxieties can be obscured. Attached, the patient presents as functioning well in both therapy and the world; the therapist feels important, competent and successful. This symbiosis feeds both parties. Sometimes I feared that my patients' improved emotional health reflected their deep attachment to me rather than having developed a deeper, healthier attachment to themselves. And so, in the termination processes, building patients' abilities to better affirm themselves and better appreciate their roles in their improved lives seemed potentially curative.

Patients expressed anger at me for retiring, for abandoning them before they had terminated or completed their journey with me. I accepted the anger, though I reframed it: I understood their anger but wondered why it focused on my retirement rather than on my not having been more effective in helping them to better hold themselves as the competent, self-actualized people they were. I suggested that that could be viewed as a form of abandonment.

After I was gone, patients would miss me, and I them. How they carried me would be important. What was ultimately most important: how they carried themselves. To get there, we addressed frequently their separation anxieties: how could they live without me? What was their resistance to holding themselves, as they wanted me to hold them? What would it look like if they cared for themselves as I cared for them?

The work stirred by my retirement with each patient was powerful and rich, even those therapies that didn't end as I had wished. Jeri came to a session about two weeks after I announced my termination to inform me that two weeks later would be her last session: she had planned a trip for the week after and saw no reason to be financially responsible for that session. (It was my impression that she planned the trip after my announcement; this gave her the control of the ending, control she relentlessly sought throughout the therapy.) Additionally, after 15 years of therapy, if she hadn't gotten what she had wanted, like meeting a man and getting married, she wasn't going to get that in the remaining four months. She wanted to leave the door open to seeing me, if I had an opening, after her trip. Though tempted, I held firm, supporting her instincts that terminating in that moment was what she needed to do. I knew any additional sessions would be frustrating to both of us. Helping her value herself as she said her good-bye as best she could seemed the most respectful ending.

Morgan utilized the remaining months to continue to process Mary's death, coming to understand it as equally tragic as the life she lived. Though he stuck to his promise—that she would have 24/7 care at home—he carried guilt that he had not felt more loving towards her. He resented that in their marriage she projected onto him her angry and unfinished work generated by her relationship with her father. In our termination, Morgan grew in his abilities to express anger at me for cancelling a session or changing the time. He challenged my interventions if he felt them wrong or off base. He wept for himself, regretting that unlike me, he had retired in poor health and was lonely.

Over many years, Morgan created paper sculptures, which he treasured. In the months prior to my announcement, he started giving away pieces to people important to him, people whom he feared he might not see again before he died. In his therapy, he talked extensively about his process of selecting which piece went to whom. We explored what was necessary in the experience for him to get something back for himself in the giving. In our final month, he enacted in our relationship what he had integrated from this work.

When I arrived at his home for a session, I was directed to his studio. He was waiting for me with a number of his sculptures displayed. He wanted us, together, to select a piece for me. In our last sessions, we discussed what different pieces represented and ultimately selected the piece that for Morgan best represented his growth in our journey. He described the piece as "raw and stark, reminding me to not be frightened of my emotions."

As sculpture helped frame Morgan's ending, ballet helped frame Tom's. Tom, 60 years old, had begun therapy with me about three years earlier, after having terminated a long-term therapy that he described as "having saved my life." As Tom and I began talking about my leaving, he identified profound unfinished business with his previous therapist. In that therapy, he set a date to leave; he left the "hard work until the end," setting it up to walk out on work he was frightened to explore. He resisted any input from his therapist, insisting on keeping his termination date. That unfinished work became our work.

About three weeks before our ending, Tom began focusing more specifically on our good-bye. He came to the session with his laptop, having downloaded the New York City Ballet dancing "Jewels," choreographed by George Balanchine. Together we watched a movement, after which he turned to me, in tears. Tom told me he had believed Balanchine to be the world's finest choreographer, until he worked with me. He reflected on my "brilliance in choreographing" his therapy so that he had the courage to take risks he never imaged he could take. He "never imagined" he would feel so good about himself. He appreciated my consistent encouragement that he work on the ending throughout the 5 months and not just the last weeks. This, to him, was an example of my skills as a choreographer.

Taking in Tom's expressions competed with feelings stirred by watching "Jewels" with him. Though I had seen the ballet danced before, never had I attended to the subtle strength displayed by the male dancers against the backdrop of the dominating performances by the female dancers. It was the male's strength and stability that made possible the female performances. This paralleled my perception of Tom: It was his strength, understated but dependable and reliable, that encouraged people close to him to function as effectively as they did. The richness of our remaining seven sessions continued, this co-creation satisfying and joyful to each.

Closings: Part 2

In groups, expressions of loss, sadness, helplessness, and grief dominated the processes. The last session of a women's group that I singly led for 35 years reflected the sentiments expressed throughout my practice that last week. On select occasions the group would coordinate in-group celebrations. On the occasion of my retirement this did not occur. Dreading the last session, the group resisted talking about what they wanted for themselves.

Yet, on that day, each member spontaneously brought to group something special and unique. Each offering reflected personal sentiments as well as a piece of the group expression regarding our ending. The group's synergy was exquisite. For example, one person brought orange juice, because "like therapy, it gets me going", while another person brought champagne "to celebrate what Elly has helped each of us to accomplish." One patient consciously brought nothing concrete, only her tears of joy and sadness: joy for my having pushed her to commit to the group and for having been a part of its riches; sadness that it took her so long to agree to group membership and now it was time to say good-bye. A fourth group member brought royal blue bracelets for each person, embossed with "WWES?" With little discussion members knew the letters stood for "What Would Elly Say?" Spontaneously they erupted, "Take good care. I know you have the heart and skills to do it." And so we parted.

A Year Later

I finished this piece almost a year to the date that I posted the notice, "Closed for Business." During the year when I attempted to write, my mind shut down, my body ached, and words were elusive. Mourning the losses stirred by my retirement filled the space. Do I still think about my patients? Absolutely. Have I had any contact with them? A few called me for a referral and others sent me birthday greetings. Do I miss the work? Definitely. Do I miss frequent collaboration with colleagues? Unequivocally.

Do I regret having retired? NO. I like myself more now. I am calmer, gentler, kinder, and more relaxed. After living the life I lived for 40 years, its intensity, pace, and pressure had become second nature to me, and at 70, I underestimated its cost. Should I have reduced my practice to work less? No. I loved doing psychotherapy the way I did it, with the intensity that seeing patients multiple times a week permitted. I appreciate my courage in retiring from the work that I cherished and confronting the growth pains induced by retiring.

Most important, my initial resolve to ensure meaningful terminations for my patients and me provided an opportunity for profound psychotherapy. The experience of living in the truth that nothing lasts forever and having an opportunity to do the therapeutic work stimulated by that, provided deep professional experiences that could not be replicated, experiences of a lifetime.

I am still young in this life stage, learning to appreciate the wisdom accrued during my rich professional life. What lies ahead? I don't know, trusting it will evolve over time. As my close friends and I learn about growing our friendships deeper in the absence of our days being more similar, parts of my character, long hidden, slowly emerge. In this struggle I continue to grow and my life becomes richer. I believe this to be the conduit for who I was and who I will grow to be. ▼

Memory, Meaning & Story:
Understanding Our Narratives and Changing Our Scripts
Voices, Spring 2019

Call for Papers

WE ALL TELL OUR STORIES: OF WHO WE ARE, FROM WHENCE WE CAME, OF LIFE EVENTS THAT SHAPED AND TURNED OUR DIRECTIONS. We tell stories of relationships, attachments, and encounters—what happened, who said or did what and why—recounting gifts or grievances received with lasting impact. Sometimes those stories are drawn from clear memories, well grounded in what actually happened. Sometimes our "memories" are more family lore, shaped by the stories we were told of events we were too young to remember or inherited from our ancestors, written before our time. Other times, the stories are built from screen memories, compiled from a mix of experiences, interpretations, and ascribed meanings, scripted into narratives drawn tight around us as if it all happened just so—and will always be just so.

Deadline for submission:
January 15, 2019
Direct questions and submissions to the editor, Carla Bauer, LCSW
crbauer01@bellsouth.net

See Submission Guidelines on the AAP website:
www.aapweb.com.

What are the stories of your life, of your sense of self? What are the relationships and attachments that shaped you? The experiences that defined you or turned your course? The roles you wear as if your life or family depended on it? What are the wounds you've built protective walls around? What messages and experiences have you absorbed into your sense of self: e.g., "You're lazy," or "You're too needy;" "I'm invisible," or "I deserve pain"? What are the narratives you don like a well-worn jacket and find yourself living out repeatedly? Do you feel stuck in an immutable script, doomed for endless repetition? Or have you had experience with rewriting the narrative, rescripting your future course?

For this issue of *Voices*, consider the roles of memory, meaning and story in defining and changing life scripts. Consider your own narratives and those of your clients, the stories told in your offices. How do memory, meaning and story intertwine to shape the narratives and scripts of our lives/selves and hold us in their grip? How do we help clients make sense of their narratives and shift their meanings, exchanging the historical script for a new storyline? Object relations, narrative therapy, internal family systems, and more—each theoretical orientation gives us a different lens on the link between past and present, via the interrelationship of memory, meaning and story. What have you found useful in understanding narratives and changing scripts—yours or those of your clients? What has not been helpful?

Voices welcomes submissions in the form of personal essay, research- and case-based inquiry, poetry, art, cartoons and photography. ▼

Call for Papers

The Ghost in You:
Psychotherapy and the Art of Grieving
Voices, Summer 2019

> "Embrace your grief, for there your soul will grow."
> —Carl Jung

Deadline for submission:
April 15, 2019
Direct questions and
submissions to the editor,
Carla Bauer, LCSW
crbauer01@bellsouth.net

See Submission
Guidelines on the AAP
website:
www.aapweb.com.

LOSS IS INTEGRAL TO THE HUMAN EXPERIENCE. There is no attachment without the risk and eventuality of loss. The response to loss, however, determines our engagement in the present moment. The ability to navigate grief helps determine the quality and duration of our relationships. Mourning can be a vehicle for, or an obstacle to, growth.

Therapeutic witnessing offers a unique opportunity to metabolize grief, and the echoes of past loss can be a cry to reawaken to life. However, for the therapist and the patient whose unresolved grief has been touched, the work may be excruciating and can create unintended impasses. Dissociation, repression, fragmentation, and somatization can all vie for control. Ultimately, the goal is to integrate and regulate, rather than exorcise, haunted histories.

Consider the theme of grief and ghosts as it relates to the person of the therapist, the therapy process, our community, and the world at large. How do productive responses to loss and grief facilitate growth and development? How do ghosts interfere with mourning and haunt the therapy process? How do dissociation, fragmentation, repression, and somatization inhibit grief work? How does unresolved grief contribute to intergenerational transmission of trauma, haunting individuals, institutions, and communities? How do cultural differences in the understanding of death and grieving rituals impact the metabolism of loss?

Some potential areas of grieving ghosts, in both clients and therapists: relatives and survivors of holocaust and other cultural traumas, conscious and unconscious; illness, aging, death; disabled or ill children; divorce (marital, friendship, co-therapy); life transitions (college, moving away, marriage, retirement); political grief; decision making, commitment, and loss of freedom; group therapy grief (illness, termination); incarceration.

What ethical concerns arise around confidentiality, boundaries, disclosure and other matters when loss and grief enter the therapy relationship? How does attending to the ghosts within our clients trigger our own experiences of loss, and how do the losses in our lives trigger the ghosts within our clients?

Voices welcomes submissions in the form of personal essay, research- and case-based inquiry, poetry, art, cartoons and photography.

The Geometry of Place, The Tangled Roots of Home
Voices, Winter 2019

Call for Papers

OUR HISTORIES OF PLACE AND HOME ARE SHARED BY FAMILY AND COMMUNITY AND ARE UNIQUE-LY PERSONAL AT THE SAME TIME. This issue of Voices will explore how the physical, emotional, and psychological dimensions of place and home shape and hold us and make us uniquely who we are as human beings.

Consider: What does the construct of "home" mean to you? How did the landscape of your childhood shape your identity, your psyche, and the rhythms of your life? How did the place you were raised inform your understanding of reality and your values? How did your roots impact your journey into the world beyond home? What has been your experience of leaving home or finding and forming "home" throughout your life? How has your own experience of place and home influenced the milieu you have created or adopted for your work as a therapist?

Consider also the ways in which your clients' unique histories of place and home have shaped their journey, their struggles, and their sense of safety and belonging. How do their histories affect and inform your therapeutic endeavors and your relationship to your clients, whose trajectories toward and away from home inevitably differ from your own?

Voices welcomes submissions in the form of personal essay, research- and case-based inquiry, poetry, art, cartoons and photography.

▼

Deadline for submission:
August 15, 2019
Direct questions and submissions to the editor, Carla Bauer, LCSW
crbauer01@bellsouth.net
or to the guest editors.
See Submission
Guidelines on the AAP
website:
www.aapweb.com

Winter 2019
Guest Editors:
David Pellegrini, PhD
dspellegrini@gmail.com
Tom Burns, PhD
burnsvoices@gmail.com

Subscribe to Voices

The American Academy of Psychotherapists invites you to be a part of an enlightening journey into…

VOICES

Voices is a uniquely rewarding publication providing a meeting ground with other experienced psychotherapists. A theme-oriented journal, *Voices* presents personal and experiential essays by therapists from a wide range of orientations. Each issue takes you on an intimate journey through the reflections of therapists as they share their day-to-day experiences in the process of therapy. *Voices'* contributors reveal insights inherent in our lives, our culture and our society.

As a subscriber, you'll have the opportunity to experience contributions from noted luminaries in psychotherapy. Using various styles from articles to poems, *Voices* is interdisciplinary in its focus, reflecting the aims and mission of its publisher, the American Academy of Psychotherapists.

VOICES SUBSCRIPTION

Please start my one-year subscription to AAP's journal *Voices* at $65 for individuals PDF only; $85 for individuals PDF & print copy. Institutional subscriptions may be reserved directly through the AAP office or through the traditional subscription agencies at $249 per year. *Voices* is published electronically three times per year and is delivered to your email address as an ePublication.

Name

Address

City   State   ZIP

Telephone   Fax

Email

❏ My check made payable to AAP *Voices* is enclosed.
❏ Please charge to my credit card, using the information I have supplied below:
Form of payment: ❏ Master Card   ❏ Visa
Account #   Expiration:
Signature

Address all orders by mail to:
Voices
230 Washington Ave Ext, Suite 101
Albany, NY 12203
You may also fax your order to (518) 240-1178.
For further information, please call (518) 694-5360

Guidelines for Contributors

Voices: The Art and Science of Psychotherapy, is the journal of the American Academy of Psychotherapists. Written by and for psychotherapists and healing professionals, it focuses on therapists' personal struggles and growth and on the promotion of excellence in the practice of psychotherapy. The articles are written in a personalized voice rather than an academic tone, and they are of an experiential and theoretical nature that reflects on the human condition.

Each issue has a central theme as described in the call for papers. Manuscripts that fit this theme are given priority. Final decision about acceptance must wait until all articles for a particular issue have been reviewed. Articles that do not fit into any particular theme are reviewed and held for inclusion in future issues on a space available basis.

Articles. See a recent issue of *Voices* for general style. Manuscripts should be double-spaced in 12 point type and no longer than 4,000 words (about 16 to 18 pages). Do not include the author's name in the manuscript, as all submissions receive masked review by two or more members of the Editorial Review Board. Keep references to a minimum and follow the style of the *Publication Manual of the American Psychological Association, 5th ed.*

Submit via email, attaching the manuscript as a Word document file. Send it to Kristin Staroba *(kristin.staroba@gmail.com).* Put "Voices" in the email's subject line, and in the message include the author's name, title and degree, postal address, daytime phone number, manuscript title, and word count. Please indicate for which issue of *Voices* the manuscript is intended.

If a manuscript is accepted, the author will be asked to provide a short autobiographical sketch (75 words or less) and a photograph that complies with technical quality standards outlined in a PDF which will be sent to you.

Neither the editorial staff nor the American Academy of Psychotherapists accepts responsibility for statements made in its publication by contributors. We expect authors to make certain there is no breach of confidentiality in their submissions. Authors are responsible for checking the accuracy of their quotes, citations, and references.

Poetry. We welcome poetry of high quality relevant to the theme of a particular issue or the general field of psychotherapy. Short poems are published most often.

Book and Film Reviews. Reviews should be about 500 to 750 words, twice that if you wish to expand the material into a mini-article.

Visual Arts. We welcome submissions of photographs or art related to the central theme for consideration. Electronic submissions in JPEG or TIFF format are required. If you would like to submit images, please request the PDF of quality standards from Mary de Wit at *md@in2wit.com* or find it on *www.aapweb.com.* Images are non-returnable and the copyright MUST belong to the submitting artist.

Copyright. By submitting materials to *Voices* (articles, poems, photos or artwork), the author transfers and consents that copyright for that article will be owned by the American Academy of Psychotherapists, Inc.

American Academy of Psychotherapists

VISION STATEMENT

Our vision is to be the premier professional organization where therapeutic excellence and the use of self in psychotherapy flourish.

MISSION STATEMENT

The mission of the American Academy of Psychotherapists is to invigorate the psychotherapist's quest for growth and excellence through authentic interpersonal engagement.

CORE VALUES

- Courage to risk and willingness to change
- Balancing confrontation and compassion
- Commitment to authenticity with responsibility
- Honoring the individual and the community

FULL MEMBERSHIP

Full Membership in the Academy requires a doctoral or professional degree in one of the following mental health fields: psychiatry, clinical or counseling psychology, social work, pastoral counseling, marriage and family therapy, counseling, or nursing, and licensure which allows for the independent practice of psychotherapy.

- Specific training in psychotherapy with a minimum of 100 hours of supervision.
- At least one year of full-time post graduate clinical experience (or the equivalent in part-time experience) for doctoral level applicants, at least two years for others.
- A minimum of 100 hours of personal psychotherapy.

A person who does not fulfill the above requirements but who is able to document a reasonable claim for eligibility, such as a distinguished contributor to the field of psychotherapy, may also be considered for full membership.

OTHER CATEGORIES OF MEMBERSHIP

In the interest of promoting the development of experienced psychotherapists, one category of associate membership is offered for those with the intent of becoming full members. These members will be working with a mentor as they progress to Full Membership.

Associate Membership

- has completed a relevant professional degree
- is currently practicing psychotherapy under supervision appropriate to the licensure
- has recommendations from at least three faculty, supervisors, and/or Academy members
- has completed or is actively engaged in obtaining 100 hours of personal psychotherapy
- agrees to work with an Academy member mentor
- may be an associate for no more than five years

Student Affiliate

For students currently enrolled in a graduate degree program. Application includes acceptable recommendations from two faculty, supervisors or Academy members.

For information regarding membership requirements or to request an application, contact the Central Office. Membership information and a printable application form are also available on the Academy's Web site, www.aapweb.com.

EXECUTIVE OFFICES

aap@caphill.com
230 Washington Ave Ext, Suite 101
Albany, NY 12203
Phone (518) 240-1178
Fax (518) 463-8656

2018 OFFICERS

Doug Cohen, PhD
President

Gordon Cohen, PsyD
Immediate Past President

David Donlon, LCSW
President-Elect

Steven Ingram, D Min
Secretary

Philip Spiro, MD
Treasurer

EXECUTIVE COUNCIL

2015 – 2018
Ellen Carr, MSW
Jacob Megdell, PhD

2016 – 2018
Judy Lazarus, MSW

2016 – 2019
Neil Makstein, PhD
Stephanie Spalding, LCSW
Linda Tillman, PhD

2017 – 2020
David Pellegrini, PhD
Lori Oshrain, PhD
Tandy Levine, LCSW

Made in the USA
Columbia, SC
03 October 2018